MODERN REPRINTS

THOEMMES

Printed in Great Britain by Antony Rowe Ltd, Chippenham, Wiltshire

THE PHILOSOPHY OF SCHILLER IN ITS HISTORICAL RELATIONS

Emil Carl Wilm

THOEMMES PRESS

Published in 1994 by

Thoemmes Press
85 Park Street
Bristol BS1 5PJ
England

ISBN 1 85506 330 1

This is a reprint of the 1912 Edition

Publisher's Note

These reprints are taken from original copies of each book. In many cases the condition of those originals is not perfect, the paper, often handmade, having suffered over time and the copy from such things as inconsistent printing pressures resulting in faint text, show-through from one side of a leaf to the other, the filling in of some characters, and the break up of type. The publisher has gone to great lengths to ensure the quality of these reprints but points out that certain characteristics of the original copies will, of necessity, be apparent in reprints thereof.

Preface

THE work presented here is not intended to be a technical or exhaustive treatment of Schiller's philosophy. I have sought, rather, to give an account, which would be fairly intelligible to the non-philosophical reader, of those main stages of Schiller's reflective thought, in their historical relations, an understanding of which is necessary for the complete comprehension of the great poet's character, and of his literary productions. To do this has not been a very easy task, as the reader acquainted with the character of Schiller's theoretical writings can easily imagine. It is perhaps due to the fact that I have had the literary and general student rather than the technical philosopher in mind while writing the essay that a certain lack of completeness in the scope of the work will be evident to the reader who has been accustomed to think of Schiller as a writer whose main speculative interest was in historical and æsthetical subjects. Interesting and valuable as the æsthetical writings are from a scientific point of view, they do not throw much light on the more purely literary productions upon which Schiller's fame mainly rests, and in relation to which my essay was more particularly conceived.

I have endeavored, in working out my subject, to avail myself, as far as possible, of the large and valuable literature which has accumulated about it during more than a century. I am especially indebted to the admirable treatises of Überweg, Tomaschek and Kuno Fischer. Whatever value may attach to the innovations I have made in the traditional treatment (if there be any such) it is more appropriate to call attention to the large debt I owe to these and other writers than to any inaccuracies I may have detected, or new views I may have advanced, which may commend themselves to the reader. For a good part of the present material, therefore, I claim no other merit than that of having presented it for the first time in English, and thus having made it accessible to those readers who, everything else equal, prefer the English book when it is available. I should say, however, in justice to myself, that I have never merely reproduced or translated. All the chapters have been based upon a careful and often a repeated reading of the writings under discussion.

The reader who wishes to get at the heart of Schiller's philosophy without delay can do so by omitting chapters III, IV and VI, which deal either with immature or with transitional phases of the poet's thought, and are, therefore, primarily of historical or antiquarian interest.

E. C. WILM.

HARVARD UNIVERSITY, *January, 1912.*

Contents

CHAPTER		PAGE
I.	LITERATURE AND PHILOSOPHY . . . . . The types of temperament, 1. Philosophy and literature: analogies, 3. Distinguishing features of literature: beauty of diction, 4. Its noble redundancy, 6. Literature as normative, and relation to religion, 7. The problems of Schiller's philosophy, and his relation to Kant, 8. His obscurity, 11. Aim and standpoint of the present work, 12. Chronological, 14.	1-16
II.	THE HISTORICAL BACKGROUND: LEIBNIZ AND THE BRITISH MORALISTS . . . The metaphysics of Leibniz: reality as monads or individual centres of energy, 17. Energy as rational or telic, 18. The problem of evil: optimism, 21. Ethics, 22. Virtue and happiness, 22. Shaftesbury. World harmony, 23. The primitive propensities and their organization, 24. The utility of virtue, 24. The doctrine of the moral sense, 25. Shaftesbury and Schiller, 25. Hutcheson, 26. Permanent value of the ethics of proportion, 28.	17-34
III.	EARLY VIEWS . . . . (a) *The Relation of Body and Mind: The Psychophysical Problem* The Master's dissertation, 36. General world-view, 37. The problem of body and mind, 41. Schiller's solution of the problem: *Mittelkraft,* 43. The sense organ and the organ of thought, 44. Association of ideas, 45. Attention and action, 46. The function of bodily feeling, 48.	35-68

CHAPTER PAGE

(*b*) *The Connection Between the Animal and the Spiritual Nature in Man: The Psychophysical and the Human Problem*
Relation of the two essays, 49. The function of feeling, continued, 50. Evolution, individual and social: heterogony of ends, 43. Reaction of mental states on the body, 56. Physiognomy, 57.

(*c*) *The Stage as a Moral Institution*
More modern tone of the essays, 59. The function of art, 60. The relation of the stage to religion and to law, 62. One-sidedness of the essays, 63. Summary of early views, 64.

IV. AWAKENING 69-86
The Philosophical Letters and Related Poems
The significance of the *Letters* and related poems, 69. Origin of the *Letters*, 72. Authorship and dates, 76. The attitude of feeling and the attitude of reflection, 78. Kantian influence, 82.

V. THE STUDY OF KANT 87-99
First acquaintance with the Kantian philosophy, 87. Schiller at Jena, and his relation to Reinhold, 88. Illness and philosophical studies, 92. Influence of the study of philosophy upon Schiller's poetry, 94.

VI. FIRST FRUITS 100-114
The Essays on the Tragic
Composition of the essays, 100. The function of art to please, 103. Natural and moral fitness, 106. Kantian elements in the essays, 108. The æsthetic value of tragedy, 110.

VII. INDEPENDENT DEVELOPMENT . . . 115-156
Retrospect: the fundamental motives of Schiller's philosophy, 115. The concept of beauty: freedom-in-the-appearance, 123. Beautiful conduct and the beautiful soul

CHAPTER PAGE

(*die schöne Seele*), 124. Criticism of Kant, 126. Beauty of conduct and moral worth: the merely legal and the moral, 135. The limitations of humanity: *Würde,* 145. Art and moral culture, 149.

VIII. RELATION TO POST-KANTIAN IDEALISM . 157-172
Lack of appreciation of Schiller's true metaphysical affiliations. Reasons for this, 157. Materials for the determination of his relation to Post-Kantian Idealism, 160. Contact with Fichte and relation between the two men, 161. Literary controversy between Fichte and Schiller, 164. Hegel's misconception of Schiller's philosophy, 167. Conclusion, 170.

NOTES 173

BIBLIOGRAPHY 179

The Philosophy of Schiller

CHAPTER I

LITERATURE AND PHILOSOPHY

THAT every man is born either a Stoic or an Epicurean, a remark attributed, I believe, to Mr. Lecky, is one of those facile generalizations whose attractiveness to the average man seems to depend more upon the boldness and simplicity with which it is stated than upon the actual truth which it embodies. The distinguishing trait of the Stoic mind is reason; that of the Epicurean, feeling. The fundamental impulse of the Stoic temperament is the logical impulse; that of the Epicurean, the eudæmonistic or æsthetic impulse. The former may be said to represent the universal, or the whole; the latter, the individual, the part. But as nature itself represents a curious commingling of order and eccentricity, and as social life is a peculiar product of individual and collective interests, of acquiescence to rule and of individual initiative, so man, the integral part of nature and of the social order that he is, represents in himself at his completest, as Plato long ago suggested, a mixture of passion and reason, of wilful impulse and restraint. In his outlook on life he is both poet and philosopher, dreamer and realist, prophet and seer. The deepest truth concerning life and man is not reached by the cold dialectic of the philosopher with his sense for fact and truth, nor through the emotional promptings of the poet, with his sense for harmony and beauty. Indeed, the great teachers and leaders of humanity, Job and Isaiah, Æschylus and Sophocles, Shakespeare and Browning, Goethe and Schiller, have not been poets merely, or philosophers merely, but both. Perhaps the most striking example of this composite type of character, too versatile to be forced into any convenient rubric, is Robert Browning, who, according to a widely prevalent opinion, is the most universal interpreter of our modern life, representing and reflecting in himself "its confused strength and chaotic wealth."[1] Primarily a poet, with a poet's feeling for beauty and artistic fitness, he is also a philosopher, holding a theory of life which he is ready to defend with all the resources of a lavishly endowed intellect. No other English poet lends himself more readily to poetic apprehension and interpretation; at the same time there is probably no other great

English poet whose ruling ideas are so readily disengaged from the poetic forms in which they find expression.

The commingling of poetic and philosophical elements in the works of the most representative writers is entirely natural when we remember the relations between philosophy and literature, which are more numerous and intimate than might, at first sight, seem to be the case. The problems of philosophy and literature are common problems. Both alike differ from the special sciences in the respect that they do not seek, through observation and experimental investigation, to add to the stock of knowledge already accumulated. Both differ from the special sciences in the respect that they do not confine themselves to special aspects of reality, or to particular classes of facts, but deal with experience or life in its broadest signification. Literature, no more than philosophy, can be unfaithful to the truth of things. "No great art could ever live," says the late Edward Caird, "if it ceased to regard beauty as one with truth and goodness. No poet ever touched the deepest springs of human emotion, who regarded himself as the idle singer of an empty day."[2]

Nor is the approach of philosophy and literature to their problems so different as is frequently supposed. Philosophy, for example, is often said to approach its problems by the method of purely intellectual analysis and interpretation, while literature is said to approach its problems through intuition or immediate insight, "gaining God by first leap." But, evidently, every legitimate method of reaching truth is open to philosopher and poet alike. The solution of the poet's problems probably involves vastly more intellectual labor than the highly finished product of his pen suggests. On the other hand, the thought of the gifted philosopher, like that of the poet, often leaps, lightning-like, from peak to peak of the intellectual realm, clearing many intermediate points which a less practised or powerful thinker must laboriously surmount. What Professor Santayana has so finely said of religion [3] is of course eminently true of poetry, but it is true to a large degree of philosophy as well. It too has its instinctive and blind side, "feeling its way, however, steadily toward the heart of things, and from whatever quarter it may come, veers in the direction of the ultimate." [4]

If the difference between philosophy and literature is not to be sought in the problems with which they deal, nor in the method by which they approach and deal with these problems, in what does the difference between them consist? It consists mainly, as I conceive the matter, in the form through which philosophy and literature are expressed. With philosophy, the matter is of fundamental importance: the form in which its truths are expressed is of subsidiary interest only. Not so with literature, which, as a branch of fine art, must give the truth an ideally beautiful expression. Like the clever artificer who takes a "sliver of pure gold . . . mere oozings from the mine," and subjects it to

> ". . . the file's tooth and the hammer's tap:
> Since hammer must needs widen out the round,
> And file emboss it fine with lily-flowers,
> Ere the stuff grow a ring-thing right to wear,"[5]

so the poet takes the "pure crude fact" of life, "melts up wax with honey, so to speak," and forms it into a thing of power and beauty, which is no sooner conceived than it glows and pulsates in the soul, raising its energy and swelling the tide of its life.

A leading condition of the emotional and pedagogical effectiveness of literature is of course that its exposition of truth be through the concrete rather than the conceptual, making its appeal to the imagination rather than to the logical understanding. Thus, "where truth in closest words shall fail," the

> ". . . truth embodied in a tale
> Shall enter in at lowly doors."

No doubt, the poet, with his strong sense for unity and artistic completeness, will often exceed the stricter limits of truth which philosophy sets itself. What is "left abrupt" in philosophy is often ideally completed in poetry. The poet, laboring under emotional stress, will often be tempted to thrust aside the veil that separates him from the ultimate realities which the more cautious methods of philosophy fail to disclose. And, where knowledge entirely fails, the poet, like the plain man, will "cling to the sunnier side of doubt,"[6] believing where he cannot prove. If, strictly speaking, he is guilty of untruth, it is of that noble untruth whose very appeal to man proves him to be something more than a mere child of earth, content with what earth offers.

This suggests what seems to me to be perhaps the principal office of poetry, namely to soften down the hard lines and the harsh distinctions in nature to which natural science and a mechanistic philosophy have too much accustomed us. Under the natural-scientific and mechanistic view of the world, matter, not spirit, is the sole reality, and man, and the various interests associated with his life, appear rather as incidents, important indeed for man, but entirely unimportant otherwise, in the process of universal evolution. The iron-shod universe described by natural science is one in which the higher life of man must expire for want of appropriate support and sustenance. If science has disillusioned man, it is the function of poetry to re-illusion him, and to quiet his misgivings by pointing out the unity and beauty of the world, and by giving to it an ultimately spiritual interpretation.

This suggests a second characteristic of literature which broadly differentiates it from science and philosophy. While the standpoint of the latter is primarily that of description and interpretation, the standpoint of literature is that of ethical demand as well. In this respect it closely resembles that other great interest, so closely related to both philosophy and literature, religion. Religion, too, is fundamentally a theory of life, offering an illumination of life.[7] But besides being a theory of life, religion is also a force in life. Its solution of the world problem is not theoretical merely, it is also practical. Religion is not merely speculative, it is remedial as well. It is an ethical imperative, a call to duty, a programme of salvation. So also with poetry. It declares not merely what is, but what shall be. Facing the evil and ugly aspects of reality, it recognizes them only as temporary forms, and as ideally non-existent. It acknowledges them only to condemn them. The poet is not so much a discoverer of what is, as he is a revealer and a creator of what ought to be. His will and word are productive forces, making over the mind of man, and, with it, the world.

In the writings of Schiller the literary and philosophical motives are inextricably interwoven, a circumstance completely explained by the composite character of his personality. Indeed, it would be quite impossible to gain an adequate view of Schiller's ethical thought or of the poet's significance in the development of modern ethical speculation unless the poetic quality of his temperament, and the æsthetic point of view, which was such a striking characteristic of his reflective activity, were clearly apprehended and constantly kept in view. There was in his make-up, to quote the words of a distinguished modern writer,[8] "that wonderful blending of the artistic spirit, in which lay his affinity with Goethe, and of the strenuous character, in which he resembled Fichte, and which prepared him, as it did Fichte, for the understanding of Kant." The deep vein of the heroic in his nature was tempered and refined by close contact with the Greek spirit, into which his sympathetic study of classical literature had brought him; and, while he always retained what seems almost an inspired enthusiasm for the morally heroic, he also developed that exquisite sensitiveness for the external shapes of beauty, a shock to which could not be atoned for by any act or situation, no matter how self-forgetful or sublime.

It is this quality of Schiller's genius, already discoverable in the earliest writings of his school period, but reaching greater maturity under the influence of Hellenism and of Goethe, to which must be attributed the advance upon the harsh rigorism of the ethical system of Kant which it is unquestionably the merit of Schiller to have inaugurated. For in spite of the verbal coincidence of many passages in the two men's writings, and notwithstanding the opinion of careful writers like Drobisch and Meurer, and, more recently, of Kühnemann,[9] we have not, I think, a mere reproduction in Schiller, in a more rhetorical dress, of the round of Kantian ethical conceptions, but a real advance of first importance — an advance which consists, on the psychological side, in a fuller recognition of the essential unity of human nature, of the significance and rights, in the moral life, too much neglected by Kant, of the desiderative or sensuous side of man's nature, and of the possibility of educating this to the point where it will not be the antagonist of reason, but an integral part of the complete moral character; on the moral side, in the concrete synthesis of law and end, the dutiful and the good, a synthesis which, speaking broadly, characterizes the whole trend of post-Kantian and of contemporary ethical thought. When a recent writer[10] speaks of the end of life as "an ideal of character, to be realized by the individual; and his attitude to it one of obligation to realize it . . . not something to be got or to be done but to be or to become," he but restates the favorite thought of Schiller that "man's destiny is not to perform individual moral actions, but to be a moral being; virtue, not virtues, is his task, and virtue is nothing but an inclination to duty." The ideal of the harmonious unfolding of the soul, then, as the supreme end of life, the ever memorable basic idea of Greek ethics, as Höffding calls it,[11] constitutes Schiller's contribution to modern ethical philosophy.

Nor is it in the critical insight into the defects of the Kantian ethics, and the fuller recognition of the rights and possibilities of human nature, that the main merit of Schiller lies. Through his lofty exposition, in prose and in verse, of the principles and ideals of art and morality these have become the common possession of the German people, and are destined to exert their influence wherever the knowledge of German letters extends.[12]

The somewhat dogmatic statement of the central significance of Schiller's philosophy made above may seem somewhat hazardous in view of the fact that there is perhaps no other philosophical writer in recent times whose writings have been so variously interpreted.

This variety of opinions is accounted for partly by the fact that Schiller did not always have a clear understanding with himself as to which was the higher term, beauty or sublimity of action, "grace" or "dignity." The ideal towards which he strove was "beautiful conduct" (*die schöne Sittlichkeit*), the free expression of the "beautiful soul" (*die schöne Seele*), in which the sensuous and rational natures are reconciled, and duty and inclination coincide. Yet he retains the Kantian distinction between legal and moral, and grants that occasions arise when duty and inclination do not harmonize, and when the agent, in order to meet the demands of his nature as an intelligible and moral being, must subordinate the solicitations of sense to the imperative of the moral law. In the painful struggle between sense and reason which ensues, man must act with "dignity," and so express the want of harmony as to let it be seen that the victory remains with the nobler power.

As has often been remarked by his critics, Schiller was not a systematically trained philosopher, and it would not be difficult to quote passages from different writings that would be hard to reconcile with each other. It is often at the crucial point of his argument that he expresses himself with greatest hesitation. His general style, too, is not such as to relieve the difficulties of interpretation. Rhetorical and poetic, even in his scientific writings, we miss the clear-cut definitions and sharp distinctions so indispensable to clear thought and presentation; and the vacillation of his terminology, the indefiniteness of his concepts, and the boldness of his antitheses are the source of endless trouble to the student of his philosophical writings.

Another source of confusion has been the fact that in certain of his writings Schiller often develops one line of thought to the exclusion of another, and that these writings have been taken apart from the rest and studied out of connection with the whole body of his works. It is thus that Schiller has been shown to advocate several incompatible views, and to belong to as many different parties. Now, no adequate view of his philosophy will be obtained by this method of study. The development of his views must be traced stage by stage, and each writing must be treated, not as an isolated phenomenon, and complete in itself, but as belonging both to the past and to the future, as illuminated by, and shedding light on, every other. It is this service that the present work is intended to render. It is intended to do for the whole of Schiller's philosophy what has recently been done for his æsthetics:[13] to exhibit it in its historical development. Its method is *entwickelungshistorisch:* it is the growth of Schiller's reflective genius and the evolution of his philosophical concepts, particularly with reference to the influence of Kant, that will demand our special attention. The vexing problems of the Schiller philosophy, whether Schiller changed his attitude on fundamental problems, what he regarded as the highest good, and to what extent he was influenced by the reigning philosophy, can be best understood by this method of study and presentation.

It is particularly in view of the Schiller-Kant problem that the somewhat detailed summary of Schiller's early essays will be justified. It would be difficult to say just what Schiller owed to Kant unless we knew precisely what problems occupied his mind and what attitude he took toward them before the Kantian period. Besides, it will be found that they are not without scientific significance in themselves. An extended criticism, however, of these early views will not be called for. Schiller moved, for the most part, in well beaten paths, and we may content ourselves with simple exposition, and with pointing out the sources of his inspiration on the one hand, and the bearings of the thoughts, here vaguely conceived and inadequately expressed, upon his future development, on the other. It is in the later and more independent movement of his thought that a more critical attitude will be taken, and that some evaluation, in the light of the more recent development of philosophical reflection, of the innovations proposed in the fields of morals and art, will be attempted.

It will be convenient, before we undertake the more detailed account of his philosophical works, to recall briefly the main points of Schiller's biography, and to sketch in broad outlines the principal periods in his development.

Friedrich Schiller was born in 1759 and died in 1805. His literary activity extends over about twenty-five years, — from 1780, in round numbers, until his death, — and falls into three periods, as follows: From 1780 to 1785, in which were written *Die Räuber*, *Fiesco*, *Kabale und Liebe*, the lyrics of the *Anthologie*, and the beginning of *Don Carlos;* the period of scientific activity, from 1785 to 1794, in which he abandoned poetic production almost altogether and devoted himself to the study of history and the Kantian philosophy. In this period belong, besides most of the philosophical writings, presently to be enumerated, *Don Carlos*, *Geschichte des dreissigjährigen Krieges*,

Geschichte des Abfalls der vereinigten Niederlande, and translations from the Greek. Finally, the period of his connection with Goethe, 1794-1805, in which his poetic genius reached the height of its development. Here belong his philosophical poems (*Ideendichtung*), most of his ballads, and the great dramas,—*Wallenstein, Maria Stuart, Die Jungfrau von Orleans, Die Braut von Messina,* and *Wilhelm Tell.*

With the exception of the *Ideendichtung,* the philosophical writings all fall within the first two periods of Schiller's literary activity. But it will be more convenient to consider them in three groups again, corresponding to the three stages of Schiller's philosophical development. I have distinguished a pre-critical period, extending from 1779 to, say, 1785, in which fall the two early medical essays, *Die Philosophie der Physiologie,* and *Über den Zusammenhang der thierischen Natur des Menschen mit seiner geistigen,* two dramaturgical essays, *Über das gegenwärtige deutsche Theater* and *Die Schaubühne als moralische Anstalt betrachtet,* and a few poems of philosophical significance, the *Lauraoden* and *Die Freundschaft.* Then follows a period of transition, 1785-1792, in which were written *Der Geisterseher, Die philosophischen Briefe, Der Kampf, Resignation, Die Künstler, Über den Grund des Vergnügens an tragischen Gegenständen* and *Über die tragische Kunst.* Finally, a period of criticism and independent development, 1792-1796, in which fall the essays on the Sublime and the Pathetic, *Anmut und Würde*, the *Briefe über die ästhetische Erziehung des Menschen, Über naive und sentimentalische Dichtung*, and a group of philosophical poems of which *Das Ideal und das Leben* is the most typical and the most important.

CHAPTER II

THE HISTORICAL BACKGROUND: LEIBNIZ AND THE BRITISH MORALISTS

It will be desirable, before we undertake the discussion of Schiller's pre-Kantian views, to sketch briefly the main outlines of the philosophical systems from which Schiller's earlier ideas were mainly derived. It is hoped that in the course of our study the real affiliation of Schiller's metaphysical and ethical views, both in their earlier development and in their maturest expression, will become increasingly obvious.

The lines of philosophical speculation in the seventeenth and eighteenth centuries which mainly interest us here are the optimistic rationalism of Leibniz and his school, on the one hand, and the ethics of proportion, traceable, indeed, to classic antiquity, of Shaftesbury, Hutcheson and their followers, on the other.

The leading ideas of the Leibnizian philosophy are of such intrinsic and historical importance that we shall be obliged to examine them somewhat carefully.[14] The fundamental nature of reality, according to Leibniz, is not expressible in terms of extension (materialism) nor in a double set of terms, extension and consciousness (Cartesian dualism), but in terms of activity or force. Reality exists in the form of monads, which are indivisible centers of energy, and are, accordingly, psychical rather than physical in their ultimate constitution. They are entirely independent, or non-equatable. These monads, or punctual entities, are, moreover, spontaneous in their activity. Their behavior is not due to forces impinging upon them from without; it is a constitutional trait. Monads, in the language of Leibniz, are impenetrable, that is, they are incapable of being influenced from the outside. They contain in themselves the complete ground for their changing states. Monads, that is, are not only active, they are self-active. The monads making up the body and the mind, for example, do not act upon one another when I will to raise my hand, or when a physical stimulus gives rise to a state of consciousness. Body and mind do not interact. They merely act in unison according to a pre-established harmony among all monads. To use the language of technical philosophy, there is no such thing as transeunt causality, — a compulsive force slipping out of one thing into another thing, — all causality is immanent causality.

An objection might here be raised to the apparently divisive and disrupting tendency of this theory of the ultimate supremacy of the monad. Do we not have here, the objection might run, a pluralistic universe, or, to avoid a contradiction in terms, a mere multiverse? How can we ever build a genuine universe or world out of mutually repellent, or, at any rate, independent atoms? Instead of the wonderfully contrived organism, or at least the stupendous mechanism, that we have taken the universe to be, we have here only a rope of sand, or, still worse, a host of warring elements.

This criticism, so disconcerting at first, can be successfully met by endowing the individual monad with essential rationality. It will find its rightful place within the larger whole, not by being forced into it by some extraneous power, law, or abstract reason, operating upon it from without, but in virtue of its own intrinsic rationality. *The monad has a habit of harmonious coöperation.* For this theory we have indeed in Leibniz the pregnant suggestion. Every monad, we have seen, is a psychical being because gifted with the psychical quality of appetition or will. It is a psychical being or soul for still another reason: it is gifted with perception or sentiency. Appetition or will is, in fact, only a modification of perception; it is the name for the tendency of perceptions to pass into each other. "*L'appetit est la tendance d'une perception à une autre.*"

Thus, while ideas are essentially dynamic or active, will is essentially rational in character. The universe is rational in every part. Reason does not exist in some disembodied form, external to the individual, but is immanent in the very heart of things. The reason of the whole is exhibited by each finite part, though perhaps in varying degrees of explicitness.

We have thus arrived at three far-reaching conclusions: (1) Monads, or the ultimate constituents of reality, are fundamentally characterized by activity or energy. The whole of reality is thus will or power, and the part shares in the will or power of the whole. (2) The seat of power or energy is plural or individual. The monad does not borrow its energy; it is itself the source of energy. The part shares in the freedom of the whole. (3) Reality is essentially and immanently rational. The part shares in the rationality of the whole. The monad is self-active, intrinsically rational and free.

It would, of course, be difficult to say just to what extent Schiller derived his philosophical and poetic inspiration from the profound generalizations of Leibniz which fairly dominated European philosophy until the advent of Kant. That Schiller became familiar with the salient features of the Leibnizian philosophy in the Stuttgart Academy is certain; that this philosophy was such as to prove congenial to his highly speculative intellect and his eager and freedom-loving temperament is also sufficiently obvious. At any rate, we have in the ingenious and bold generalizations of Leibniz the philosophical groundwork for all that was most characteristic in the philosophical and literary productions of the future poet of freedom: his metaphysical and practical idealism, his theory of the ethical rights of sensibility against the domination of reason, and of the rights of the individual against social and political oppression.

The doctrine of the immanence of reason in the universe is apparently contradicted by the presence of evil in the world. This difficulty Leibniz meets with the well known argument that evil exists only in the details, and that it disappears when the details are given their proper setting in the larger context of experience. The rationality of the universe, we might say, is not evident if we view the individual being in its separate life, but only if we view it as a part of the larger life of the universe in which it shares. So physical and moral evil finds its justification in that it makes for good. Like the minor strain in a musical masterpiece, it contributes to the beauty and perfection of the whole. Evil, then, is merely a finite fact, a superficial appearance. Viewed more comprehensively, its rationality and meaning are obvious. The world is the best of all possible worlds.

Although Leibniz's ethical views were not so influential as his metaphysics in the development of subsequent philosophy, they are in themselves sufficiently noteworthy, and furnish natural points of contact with the ethical system of Shaftesbury and his school, from which Schiller's ethical views were more directly drawn. Morality, according to Leibniz, is a natural growth, provided for by the tendency to activity or self-perfection inherent in every individual, as in reality everywhere. The self-perfection of the individual consists, on the intellectual side, in a striving for clearer knowledge. In man, as his enlightenment increases, the originally blind impulse, aimed at transitory pleasures of sense, will give place to an impulse to enduring delight in spiritual perfection; and, as the interdependence of all beings becomes obvious with enlightenment, the individual will seek the perfection of others as well as his own. Metaphysical insight thus contributes to the moralization and ethical perfection of man. He will perform his individual function well in proportion to his appreciation of his place in the world order.

Further, progress in intellectual insight and in goodness is connected with pleasure, and retrogression with pain. Leibniz reiterates the classic identification between goodness and happiness, and the notion, in the degenerate form of the principle of the expediency of virtue, rules the ethical thought of the entire Illumination period. The great words, enlightenment, perfection, virtue and happiness, become, in the period of intellectual sterility succeeding Leibniz, empty catchwords which are repeated with tiresome frequency until the harsh duty ethics of Kant forced men to ponder anew the ancient and profound problems for which they stood.

The concept of harmony, already in Leibniz of large metaphysical and ethical importance, is raised into even larger prominence by Shaftesbury.[15] It underlies his metaphysics, and forms the philosophical basis for his theism. It likewise determines the fundamental character of his ethical system, which was destined to become of first importance in the development of English ethics.

Order and harmony, according to Shaftesbury, characterize the universe throughout, each thing or being taking its place in a universal system. The telic character of the world, shown in the beautiful articulation of its parts, argues the existence of a power to whose formative activity the universal order must be attributed. This is the world soul, or deity. Like Leibniz, Shaftesbury finds evil only in the part. It disappears when the part is fitted into the larger context of life where it properly belongs. All apparent imperfections contribute to the perfection of the whole. The world is not only infinitely orderly, exhibiting law and reason throughout, it is also ethical in its ultimate constitution. God is infinite intelligence and power. He is also infinite love.

The notion of harmony is carried over by Shaftesbury into ethics, and rules his ethical theory throughout. Man is characterized by three kinds of primary propensities or affections, the social or natural affections, in virtue of which he takes pleasure in the well-being of others, without any ulterior aim; the self or egoistic affections, directed towards private welfare; and the unsocial affections. The latter, like hatred, envy and malevolence, are always evil. Virtue consists in the balance or harmony of the egoistic and social affections. The individual and society, this is the epoch-making thought of Shaftesbury, form an organic unit. The interest in the individual's own welfare is just as essential in the organization of man's moral nature as is the interest in the welfare of others. And, on the other hand, private welfare can be attained only as the health and welfare of the social organism becomes an object of individual care.[16]

A leading characteristic of Shaftesbury's

ethical writings, as of Leibniz's, is his insistence on the utility of virtue to the individual. This does not consist in any precarious outward advantages which might accrue to the agent, but in a permanent delight, which, though not the deliberate end of moral activity, is its essential concomitant. A state of inner blessedness is inseparable from the good life. Affection is its own reward, and ill will its own punishment.

Perhaps the most significant feature of Shaftesbury's theory is his ascription to man of the disinterested impulses, aimed at the good of the species, as a part of the original equipment of human nature, instead of deriving them from self-love, in the manner of Hobbes, Locke and their followers. This formulation of the ethical problem differs also radically from Kant's, of which more anon. In another respect, also, Shaftesbury's ethics reveals a marked divergence from Kant's. The moral character of an act is determined, according to Kant, by the criterion of abstract reason. Shaftesbury proposes instead his theory of the moral sense, a faculty akin to the æsthetic sense, in which the active or mandatory features, so prominent in Kant, are almost completely eliminated.

Goodness as a natural inclination; virtue as a harmony of man's various powers; morality as essentially a manifestation of the beautiful;

the organization of all human powers as the goal of moral progress; and the judgment of a character or a moral situation as, at least in part, an æsthetic judgment: we have found in Shaftesbury the whole round of ethical ideas which we shall later encounter in Schiller. That we have in Schiller a type of ethical theory affiliated with Shaftesbury rather than Kant seems beyond dispute, and will become more obvious as our study advances.

The Scottish Hutcheson, although supplementing Shaftesbury at important points, does not furnish many additional ideas which are of interest for our purposes, and will therefore not call for extended notice. He reiterates the doctrine of the primitive or underived character of the social impulses, viewing man as by nature a social being. He emphasizes even more prominently than did Shaftesbury the doctrine of the moral sense, a faculty of emotional response to moral situations. So much, indeed, does he stress the emotional character of this response that he represents, according to Wundt, the culmination of the ethics of feeling. "Reason has not, as the intellectual ethics supposes, any primary significance for morals; its influence is secondary, in that it teaches us how to discriminate between what is ethically valuable and what is worthless, and helps us to reach a knowledge of the moral world-order and the power and goodness of the God who preserves that order."[17]

One further point of divergence from Shaftesbury is noteworthy, and represents a deviation from the more strictly æsthetic view of his predecessor. The only object of unqualified moral approbation, according to Hutcheson, is benevolence. This generous error he carried to the point of denying that self-regard is ever morally meritorious. Morality, in other words, does not consist, as Shaftesbury had maintained, in the mere balance of egoistic and other-regarding impulses, but in the predominance of disinterested love over all other impulses. The doctrine of the disinterested character of love seems to represent a real advance on Shaftesbury, since the latter appears to rest the reasonableness of benevolence on its conduciveness to the happiness of the individual, and thus, in spite of his formal definition of virtue in terms of complete harmony, to advocate a subtle form of hedonistic theory.[18]

Hutcheson seems to have been the first writer in modern times to mention a principle which we shall encounter in Schiller, and which has come to play a leading role in the more recent development of the psychology of conduct, the principle of the heterogony of ends. "There must arise," says Hutcheson, "in consequence of our original desires, secondary desires of everything useful to gratify the primary desires. Thus, as soon as we apprehend the use of wealth or power to gratify our original desires, we also desire them. From their universality as means arises the general prevalence of these desires of wealth and power."[19] In other words, what is originally desired merely as a means, may come eventually to be desired as an end in itself.

It may not be out of place, before we leave the discussion of the historical background of Schiller's philosophical and ethical ideas, to call attention to the permanent significance of the central ethical doctrines, especially, of Leibniz, Shaftesbury and their followers.

A problem as complex as that of morality is, of course, capable of a number of different formulations. And the value of any particular ethical theory or formula must be determined in the same way as the value of any general theory is determined, by its ability to summarize most completely the phenomena of the moral life. The various schools of ethical thought which have been prevalent in the history of ethics are reducible to three fundamental types: (1) formalistic or jural ethics, which regards conformity to some law or rule, formulated by reason, by the state or by God, as the ultimate goal of conduct; (2) hedonism, which sees the end of striving in the attainment of a state of feeling, like pleasure or happiness; (3) perfectionism, which interprets the end in terms of some particular constitution of character or of personality. A favorite way of defining morality from the last point of view is to say that it consists in the proper organization of various desires and impulses of our nature. The ethical task is essentially to introduce into life organization, order, unity. In the child, or the individual of low moral development, the single impulse, acting with the intensity due to its isolation from the rest of life, carries the day. Now what moral education does is to bring the various impulses into relation with one another; to unify the otherwise fragmentary interests of life by subordinating them to some ruling ideal or purpose. The warring and divided self must yield to the conciliated self. The problem of moralization is thus a problem of organization or mutual adaptation. And this is true whether we look at the matter from the point of view of the individual merely, or from the point of view of the relation of the individual to the social organization. Society, as Plato long ago taught, is but the individual writ large. The essential problem here too is the successful adjustment of rival interests and claims. This is indeed the ever-recurring social problem. Special interests and the welfare of the whole: these are the two terms of the antithesis the resolution of which constitutes, both in the individual life and in the social and political sphere, our common and unending human task. Nor can common welfare be defined except in relation to human desire. It is still that which satisfies desire. Only desire is not now some isolated desire, detached from the larger interests of the whole; it is a universe of desires, in which each particular element gets the satisfaction belonging to it as a part of a larger whole.

If the objection is here made that reconciliation of rival interests spoken of above is not due to the voluntary coöperation of individuals, as would seem to be suggested by the metaphysics of Leibniz and the psychology of Shaftesbury, and that the stern imperative of the law must ever be resorted to in order to bring the eccentric individual into line, the reply is that this may occur as the exception, not as the rule. The moral order, if it is to have stability, must be self-sustaining; that is, it must be upheld by the active coöperation of the individuals constituting it. The perpetuation of the state, for example, depends upon the loyalty of its citizens, and law is impossible except as it receives the support of those over whom it extends.[20] The moment the social order loses the support of the majority of its members (not, of course, the numerical majority, but the faction holding the balance of power) its future is in jeopardy. The same applies to the individual. The law of reason is not, as Kant seemed to maintain, an external force, operating upon the individual from without; it must be an expression, in some sense, of the individual's nature in its entirety.

This is not the place to argue at length the comparative merits of the competing ethical views mentioned above, but some of the advantages of the theory of perfection or self-realization over the jural and hedonistic views may here be indicated. (1) It has the advantage over the formalistic or legal view, whether in the rationalistic, political or theological form, of making morality a natural and autonomous phenomenon; it is (2) a teleological form of ethics: ethics is a science of value, *Güterlehre*, a science of goods; (3) its formulation of the good is definite and intelligible, and its suggestive force is correspondingly great; (4) the good, because conceived in personal terms, has a high emotional value; (5) the good is non-competitive, and is in this respect preferable to hedonism or utilitarianism, whose goods are often more clearly unsharable; (6) it brings ethics into organic connection with logic and æsthetics, inasmuch as it interprets the good, the beautiful and the true alike in terms of inner harmony or consistency. The view thus satisfies the most fundamental of philosophical instincts, the monistic or synthetic instinct.

Two objections of a general nature are sure to be made. The first is to the individualistic character of the theory. The good, it will be said, which is proposed as the goal of action, is merely private in character. This, however, is a misunderstanding of a fundamental assumption of the theory, which is that the social or altruistic proclivities of man are essential and native traits, and that these will be included in the harmonization of character contemplated. The common good will in that way be provided for. It may, of course, be claimed, as it is by Bradley, Professor A. E. Taylor, and apparently by Sidgwick, that the egoistic and the altruistic duties are so discrepant in the acts to which they prompt, that their reduction to a common conception is impossible. There are, however, equally competent writers who do regard the reconciliation of these deep-lying traits as possible. At any rate, this is proposed by many, Schiller himself, for example, as the very task of moral education, and it would seem hazardous to limit in advance the possibilities of moral progress.[21] Our own view has been already sufficiently indicated. The case has been admirably stated by a recent writer. "The two spheres of life (the private and the common) are inseparable. The interests and the claims of the social and the individual life overlap, and are reciprocally inclusive. They are not two lives, but two sides or aspects of one undivided life. You cannot isolate the moral individual; to do so would be to de-moralize him, to annihilate his moral nature. His very life as a moral being consists in a network of relations which link his individual life with the wider life of his fellows."[22]

It may be said, in the second place, that the end proposed in the theory of self-culture is merely formal in character, and cannot therefore furnish definite guidance, or aid us in dealing with specific situations. We are not told in what precise proportions, for example, egoistic and altruistic traits are to be combined.[23] A sufficient answer to this is that the objection applies to every ethical end that has ever been proposed. We cannot expect more than merely formal guidance from any type of ethical theory. Ethics as a science cannot, in the nature of the case, deal with specific cases, but only with typical situations. Concrete guidance can be given only by the spiritual adviser who is acquainted with the special circumstances surrounding the concrete moral situation. In the absence of such special knowledge, any moral ideal or prescription must inevitably remain merely formal or general in its nature.

The view of the moral end proposed here is not by any means a novel or untried one. It has come down the history of moral philosophy through a long line of thinkers, and claims, in fact, some of the most celebrated names in the history of philosophy for its exponents. From Heraclitus of antiquity, who proclaimed the harmony of opposites as a universal aspect of things, through Socrates, Plato, Aristotle, Butler, Shaftesbury, Schiller and the modern Höffding, not to mention scores of lesser names, the theory of self-conciliation and self-development has come down in unbroken succession from the beginning of ethical reflection in Greece to our own time. And the final formulation of ethical theory, if such is ever reached, will doubtless conform to the present theory in two important respects: it will conceive of the moral good as a personal good; it will, in the second place, so define it as to recognize the rights of the individual as well as the rights of the social organism of which the individual forms an essential part. Self-assertion as well as self-surrender will find their rightful place. Tolstoi and Friedrich Nietzsche will each come into his own. Each will be seen to have proclaimed one half of the truth, the right resting with two poet-philosophers, the Greek Plato, and a kindred spirit in our newer time, the German Schiller.

CHAPTER III

EARLY VIEWS

(a) The Relation of Body and Mind: The Psychophysical Problem

When the youthful Schiller entered the Stuttgart Military Academy in January, 1773, nearly a generation after the deaths of Leibniz and Shaftesbury, the interests and ideas sketched in the last chapter had, under the name of *Aufklärungsphilosophie*, the philosophy of Enlightenment, become the common possession of the academic world of Germany, and of a large part of Europe. In fact, the characteristic ideas of Leibnizianism, often loosely combined with ideas derived from English empiricism and the Scottish moralists, were everywhere received with an avidity well-nigh unparalleled in the history of philosophical systems. Introduced into Würtemberg by Bilfinger (1693-1748), professor of philosophy at the University of Tübingen, the tradition was continued at the Stuttgart Academy by a line of excellent teachers, Böck, Plouquet and Abel, under whose tuition Schiller came during the years 1775-80. It was particularly through the eclectic Abel, a vital and inspiring teacher, according to all accounts, that Schiller received the main stimulus to philosophical reflection.[24]

The essay, *Philosophie der Physiologie*,[25] represents Schiller's first attempt to work his way through some of the problems typical of his time, and, with the paper to be discussed next in order, which is really a re-statement and a continuation of this essay, forms the most important source for our knowledge of the poet's early speculation. The essay dates from the year 1779, and was offered as a master's dissertation to the faculty of the Stuttgart Academy. The subject was chosen by Schiller himself, and the document may therefore be regarded as representing the true bent of his mind, and the free expression of the views matured under the influence of his philosophical and medical studies in the Academy. To what extent Schiller drew upon his reading and to what extent we have the results of independent reflection; in how far the views suggested or expressed here are found in his later writings, are important questions for the student of Schiller's philosophical development, and will be constantly kept in mind during the discussion of these early writings. It will appear that the germs of much of his later philosophy were already contained in the writings of the pre-Kantian period, and that the stream of his thought, rising from many sources, was only clarified and deepened, rather than directed into other channels, by contact with the Critical Philosophy.

The essay [26] opens with reflections which at once reveal Schiller's philosophical kinship. The universe, he declares, is a divine work of art, and it is in fathoming the world-plan that man finds his true destiny, which consists in his enlightenment and perfection. And quoting almost word for word from Garve's translation of Ferguson's *Moral Philosophy*, a text-book used in the Military Academy, he adds that the soul which thus dwells in the contemplation of the plan of divine providence will be supremely happy. For, according to an eternal law, perfection and happiness, imperfection and pain, are indissolubly bound together. But another beautiful and wise law, he continues, drawing heavily upon the fourth part of Ferguson's *Moral Philosophy*, has bound the perfection of all to the happiness of each, and this with the sole purpose of advancing human kind toward its perfection and goal, which, he repeats, is "the comprehension and admiration of the great plan of nature." And here he closes these opening reflections with a significant sentence to the effect that even the pleasures of sense, though they appear to lead through devious paths and seeming contradictions, finally lead man to his true destiny, *i. e.*, to perfection and happiness.[27] There are no fundamental contradictions in the universe: happiness, virtue and perfection are identical; the whole is a grand harmony which even the pleasures and inclinations of sense can not disturb, but even these must be an integral part of the harmonious whole. In this sentence, and in the idea running throughout this whole opening paragraph, of the perfection of man through contemplation of the divine work of art, the universe, we have the beginning, however vaguely expressed, of all Schiller's subsequent ethical and artistic striving. It was his feeling for the completeness, the organic unity of the whole of nature, in which there could be no devious byways leading to irrationality, no fundamental and irreconcilable contradictions, which led him nearly fifteen years later to raise his voice against the dualism and the ascetic rigorism of the Kantian morality. Inclination and duty, sense and reason, powers which nature has joined together, had been artificially forced asunder; and it is in the reassertion of the fundamental unity of these fundamental opposites, in championing the rights of human nature in its entirety, that Schiller's main significance lies. Schiller had throughout his life two great theoretical interests, ethics and æsthetics. They are both manifested in these early and somewhat immature attempts, and the lines of his development are clearly indicated. They find their complete expression in the two typical works of his prime, the essay on *Grace and Dignity* and the *Æsthetic Letters.*

After defining his general position on philosophical problems, his *Weltanschauung* in the large, he passes somewhat abruptly to the subject proper of his dissertation, the relation of mind and body. The student of Schiller versed in the history of philosophy will at once notice that the problem presented itself to Schiller essentially in the form bequeathed to philosophy by Descartes, rather than by his more profound successor Leibniz. Descartes' historical significance in the history of psychophysics consists, as every one knows, in having clearly formulated the problem of the relation between mind and body, not in having satisfactorily solved it. The various special forms of reality which we encounter in the world cannot be reduced to a common denominator, according to Descartes, as we have already seen. There are, according to him, ultimately two forms of existence, which are essentially unequatable and irreducible, namely matter and mind. The bottom properties of these entities, extension and thought, are so discrepant in their nature that the merging of these entities into each other, or into some third and more fundamental entity, would seem to be impossible. Leibniz, however, as we have also seen, refused to accept this antithesis of matter and mind as final. To the Cartesian dualism of extended and unconscious substance, on the one hand, and inextended and conscious substance, on the other, he opposed his theory of monads, inextended and more or less conscious substances. The essence of all reality is force or will, and what we call matter is really immaterial in its ultimate essence.

Schiller, however, does not seem to have profited from the teaching of Leibniz, but, in common with the great majority of thinkers of his time, he took the Wolffian interpretation of Leibniz for his starting point, an interpretation which on this and on other points missed the very gist and genius of the teachings of the master, and which carried philosophy directly back into the dualism of Descartes.

On the properly metaphysical question of the relation between matter and spirit, it might be said here, Schiller seems never to have changed his views. On this point he was from the beginning and remained to the end a loyal follower of Kant.[28] In what respect he introduced unity into the Kantian system we have already indicated, and shall see in detail when we come to study the independent development of Schiller's thought.

At any rate, the terms in which Schiller here states the psychophysical problem completely duplicate the Cartesian distinctions. The fundamental difference between matter and mind, he says, is that matter occupies space and is impenetrable, while mind is non-spatial in character. Once stated in these terms, a monistic theory of the universe can obviously be arrived at in only two ways. One can either reduce mind to a mere form or manifestation of matter, or he can, on the other hand, interpret matter as an idea of the mind, a mental concept. If neither of these views is adopted, the only resource is to leave the two entities side by side; in other words, to abandon altogether a monistic view of the world, and frankly accept dualism. Now Schiller is clearly aware of the first two alternatives, and he as clearly rejects them, putting himself squarely on the side of metaphysical dualism.

The problem now arises, of course, how two substances so disparate can be related to each other. Is the relation merely one of parallelism, *i. e.*, do the two entities merely lie side by side, without exerting any mutual influence, like two clocks running side by side, and connected only by a preëstablished harmony? Such a thing would be indeed conceivable, but it would be inconsistent with the conception of the universe as a coherent and purposive whole. Under such a conception the course of mental events would be determined from the outside; "freedom and moral development would be a delusion, and my happiness a dream." The only other possibility is that of occasionalism, a theory of some of the Cartesians, according to which the connection between matter and mind would be mediated by God. "God intervenes on occasion of every volition, in order to excite in our bodies the movement which the soul cannot communicate to it of itself, and on occasion of each corporeal excitation, in order to produce the corresponding perception in the soul. Our volitions are the occasional causes, God the efficient cause, of our movements; the sense-objects are the occasional causes, God the efficient cause, of our perceptions."[29]

The criticism which Schiller passes upon this curious theory would have done credit to a more mature theologian than this youthful student of medicine. Under this view, Schiller remarks, each of my ideas would be a miracle, and natural law would be set aside. So far from exalting the deity by such a doctrine, we only degrade him; for the necessity of miraculous interference betrays a defect in the design, and an imperfection in the designer. He would be great, but not infinite. In short, the theories of materialism, subjectivism, preëstablished harmony, and occasionalism contradict either fundamental principles or the plain facts of experience.

A different solution from any of these must be sought. There must be a substance which occupies an intermediate position between matter and spirit, a substance which is susceptible of being acted upon by the material world, and which can in turn act upon spirit, a substance at once penetrable and impenetrable, material and spiritual. Schiller is not troubled to give a more complete determination of this mysterious somewhat. He calls it *Mittelkraft*, an intermediate agent or force; he suggests several hypotheses concerning it, as well as some difficulties; he even grants that it is inconceivable. But he dismisses all his doubts with a word: Experience proves its existence, and no amount of theorizing can contradict the plain facts of experience.

It is hardly necessary to say that the hypothesis of an intermediate agent by the interpolation of which Schiller so confidently proposes to solve the time-honored psychophysical problem, "the Great Bad" in metaphysics, as it has been called, is not original with our author, as might be inferred from his fearless appeal to the testimony of experience, by which he meant nothing more nor less than the testimony of his medical and philosophical teachers. Descartes had had his "animal spirits," which, coursing through the brain and nerves, gave rise to ideas in the mind on the one hand, and to motions of the limbs on the other. The idea of "nerve spirit" played an important part in the physiological writings of Haller, the greatest physiologist of the time; Galenus had spoken of vital spirits, and Schiller's favorite teacher, Abel, discussed the nature of this mysterious substance at length in two psychological treatises published seven years later, describing it as a "certain firelike, spiritual substance related to electric or magnetic energy." Conclusive proof as to the source of Schiller's wisdom is another dissertation of the same year, written by another pupil of Abel's, which is taken up almost exclusively with discussing and illustrating the "intermediate essence which unites the simple with the manifold, the corporeal with the non-corporeal." [30]

But the intermediate agent is not yet able to establish direct communication between such disparate terms as the physical world and the soul. The forces of the external world, such as light, sound, etc., are very diverse in their nature and in the manner of their operations. Nature has accordingly provided another set of intermediate organs in the five senses, each suited in its structure and function to the kind of physical influence it is to receive. Here Schiller introduces a distinction which anticipates one of the most vexing problems of modern physiology, the problem of the relation of the physical process in the external world to the nervous process within the nervous system, or, put differently, the question as to what modification the physical stimulus undergoes in its passage through the sense organs and other structures of the nervous system. The sense organs, Schiller observes, are of two kinds, according as the "object" undergoes modification in its transmission through the media of the sense organs, or reaches the *Mittelkraft* unchanged. The first class comprises the senses of sight, hearing and taste; the second those of smell and touch.[31] Through these media the external world is able to throw its image upon the soul. This image or representation forms the basis of all mental life. All higher knowledge, the young empiricist would seem to say, is only an elaboration of materials received through the medium of the physical senses.

Images of objects, however, would disappear with their external causes were there not some provision for their preservation, and thought, in the proper sense, could never occur. For thinking means comparing (*Gegeneinander-*

halten), bringing the representations furnished by sense perception into relations with each other. This is accomplished through another organ in which the fleeting impressions of sense are held fast and stored, as it were, in a common receptacle. This is the sensorium or the organ of thought, the microcosm in which the great world, in so far as it has been the object of sense perception, finds its counterpart.

Here Schiller plunges headlong into certain philosophical difficulties involved in the association of ideas. Ideas, of course, do not lie side by side in the mind, like so many bricks in a wall, the subject being conscious of all of them at once. They rather run their course according to certain laws of association, so that the ideas before consciousness tend to call up others related to them in certain specific ways. Now the interesting question arises, Is the flow of ideas determined by the mechanical action of the brain, or has the soul the ability to direct or control the stream of thought independently of brain action? If we adopt the mechanical theory of association, then the will, which depends upon ideas, would not be free. Freedom can be rescued only by attributing to the soul some power to control the course of consciousness. This power the soul possesses in the power of *attention*, in virtue of which certain ideas are isolated and emphasized, while others are repressed or sufficiently weakened to be robbed of their efficiency in determining action. The processes of mental combination, abstraction, retention and will are all alike possible through voluntary attention.

The importance of attention in guiding perception and in controlling the higher synthetic processes and the will, which, so far as the present writer is aware, was first clearly brought out and emphasized in this fragment of Schiller's, has in more recent psychology received very full recognition. Not only is "the degree of apperception not to be measured according to the strength of the external impression, but according to the subjective activity by which the consciousness is applied to a definite stimulus,"[32] so that the material furnished by sense impression is largely determined by the subjective activity which applies the consciousness to this or that sense stimulus, but the subjective activity manifested in the effort of attention is proposed as the essential phenomenon of the will. "The essential achievement of the will . . . is to *attend* to a difficult object and hold it fast before the mind. . . . It is a mere physiological incident that when the object is thus attended to, immediate motor consequences should ensue. . . . Though the spontaneous drift of thought is all the other way, the attention must be kept strained on that one object until at last it grows, so as to maintain itself before the mind with ease. This strain of the attention is the fundamental act of will." [33]

But man is not merely rational; he is also an emotional being. He not only receives external impressions, but he feels his inner states. The rational nature and the emotional nature are most intimately connected, the former depending largely on the latter. In keeping with the general view expressed in the opening paragraphs of the essay, feeling is given a purely teleological significance. It is that state of the soul by means of which it is conscious of its well-being or the opposite. What makes for my well-being and perfection pleases and attracts me; what makes me less perfect pains and repels me; for according to the law we so well know, happiness and perfection are one and the same. The melodious, the beautiful, minister to my interest more than the unmelodious and the ugly. What, then, is the significance of æsthetic objects in human life? But just at this point, where we promised ourselves the most valuable finds in our search for the beginnings of Schiller's later and most important thoughts, the fragment abruptly terminates.

(b) *On the Connection between the Animal and the Spiritual Nature in Man: The Psychophysical and the Human Problem*

We have observed that the essay *Über den Zusammenhang der thierischen Natur des Menschen mit seiner geistigen* is a continuation, and doubtless a repetition, of the general line of thought developed in the fragment and the lost portions of the one just considered. The importance of the senses for the mental life is reëmphasized, and their influence in "modifying and refining the changes in the world of matter" is again alluded to. The significance of the power of attention is also recalled, and there is throughout the same theologico-ethical point of view, according to which the world is a divine work of art, to fathom which is man's highest vocation and happiness. There is, however, a modification of statement and a shifting of emphasis in the repetition of the latter proposition which is perhaps worthy of notice. "Since between the measure of a power and the end toward which it works there must exist the completest harmony," *the perfection of man will consist in the highest possible activity of his powers,* and, at the same time, in their mutual subordination, in the observation of the plan of the world. To see in this sentence a closer approximation to the æsthetic point of view, and an effort toward a clearer formulation of future theory, as some writers have done, is perhaps straining a point. Certainly the terminology is neither new nor strange. That there is a "harmony between the measure of a power and the end toward which it works" is no more than Leibniz had said; Mendelssohn had seen in activity the very essence of reality, and Ferguson-Garve had made the progress of evolution toward its goal dependent upon the activity of the powers immanent in the universe.[34] But the fact that the phrasing is adhered to in later repetitions of the thought shows that the change was not made unconsciously, but marks a real advance in the formulation of the favorite thought of Schiller's early reflection.

But we have here not merely a clearer and more articulate formulation of the former views; there is also an advance to new problems. While in the *Philosophy of Physiology* the author discusses the possibility and the manner of psychophysical interaction, here, as Tomaschek points out,[35] he assumes the fact of interaction, and considers more explicitly the significance of that fact in human life.

When we come to consider the comparative importance which has been attributed to body and mind, he observes, we find that men have erred in assigning too great significance to the latter and too little to the former. Two views have prevailed: some have regarded the body as the prison-house of the spirit, checking its flight toward perfection, while others have treated knowledge and virtue only as means to happiness, and have held that the whole perfection of man consists in the amelioration and perfection of the body.[36] Both views are one-sided. But inasmuch as the latter has not seldom been cast out with over-fanatical zeal, and the mental powers have often been treated in an exclusive way, *i. e.*, in independence of the body, which is accorded a subordinate position, the author undertakes to champion the rights of that part of our nature which has been underrated, and to show, by appealing to the history of the individual and of the race, "the remarkable contributions of the body to the activity of the soul, and the great and real influence of the system of animal sensations upon the spiritual life." [37] And this is as little Epicureanism as the adoption of virtue as the highest good is necessarily Stoicism. By "animal sensations" the author means simply bodily feelings, and we are back at the point of the discussion where the essay of the preceding year terminates.

Feeling, as we saw above, has a primarily teleological significance, and is defined in teleological terms. Its function is twofold: self-preservation and the development of the mental and spiritual powers. The feelings of pain serve as warnings against the countless unfavorable influences by which the human organism is surrounded, and which threaten its destruction.

This self-protective function of feeling will, no doubt, be conceded by all. But when we inquire whether the animal nature has any higher function than that of self-preservation, objections will immediately arise. "Beyond this point," the objection will run, "the body is but the soul's inert companion, with which she must sustain a constant battle, whose pleasures reduce men to the level of the beasts, and which subjects them to a slavery from which death only can deliver them." But this is shown to be a great error when we consider the part bodily feelings actually play in the development of man's spiritual powers.

Let us imagine, says Schiller, the abstract case of a spirit out of all connection with body and hence without the feelings of bodily pleasure and pain. How would such an imaginary being conduct itself? Plainly, it would not conduct itself at all, for if it is to act it must act with some end in view, *i. e.*, it must desire, and to desire means simply to seek to obtain pleasure or escape pain. Without pleasure and pain, then, no desire, and without desire no volition and no activity.

Not only activity, but thought itself is conditioned by feeling. For what will determine the spirit to think unless it be the pleasurable sensation arising from the activity of the powers of thought? Unless we are to suppose that the spirit has been active from all eternity, it will forever remain inactive, just as a machine, unless set in motion by a power from without, will remain forever motionless. "But let the soul be placed in the condition of physical pain. Now we have feeling, the only thing which was wanting before. The transition from pain to aversion is a fundamental law of the soul. Now the will is active, and the activity of a single power is sufficient to set all the rest in motion."[38]

The general law of development of conscious life thus arrived at by abstract considerations is confirmed by observation of the development of the individual and the race. The child in its earliest years simply feels pleasure and pain; in youth we have already reflection, but reflection directed only to the satisfaction of the animal impulses and in the service of the physical body. The spiritual powers are valued only as means to an animal end. But as the youth approaches manhood the means come to be valued for their own sake. "Through frequent repetition of an activity it becomes itself a source of pleasure. The agent is delighted by the manifestation of his power, and this feeling gives him an inclination for the object which had heretofore been only a means. Enlightenment and an increase of ideas finally reveal to him the whole dignity of spiritual delights. The means has become the highest end."

The history of the individual is repeated in the history of the race. In the beginnings of civilization man's wants were few and directed only to the alleviation of his physical existence and the preservation of the species. Driven by the pangs of hunger and by exposure to the elements, he hunts, fishes, tills the soil and builds himself shelter. What knowledge there is is of a practical kind; it develops under the stress of physical necessity, and stands in the service of the physical life. The sexual instinct prompts man to the establishment of the family, the instinct of self-preservation leads to the formation of clans and tribes for purposes of common defence, the conflict of instincts brings tribes into collision with one another, and wars prompt inventions, and furnish the conditions for the development of adventurers, heroes and despots. "Cities are fortified, states organized, and with states arise civic duties and rights, the arts and industries, laws, priests and — gods."[39] Knowledge, formerly pursued only for physical ends, is now pursued for its own sake. The instinct of curiosity now serves the same end as was formerly served by the pressure of physical necessity. With leisure the sciences arise, superstition is crushed, and philosophy smiles at human folly. The influence of art and the beautiful on manners and morals is already here emphasized in a significant and well known passage: "Artists learn to imitate the works of nature, music softens the savage breast, beauty ennobles morals and taste, and art leads man to science and to virtue."[40]

From all this appears the folly of underrating our bodily nature and of endeavoring to crush out the animal feelings and instincts. "Man had to be an animal before he could be a spirit; he had to crawl in the dust before he could, like Newton, dare the flight through the universe. Without the body no activity, and without sense no perfection."[41]

In this connection may be quoted another passage which Schiller takes from Garve, and which indicates clearly two tendencies of his later development, the naturalistic tendency in ethics and æsthetics and the attitude of healthy optimism which, in spite of the stress and adversity of Schiller's life, he never permanently abandoned.

When man has once learned that nature did not awaken instincts and impulses in him simply to gratify them, that his end is not the pleasure of gratification but the activity of his powers and self-perfection, "then everything, whether animate or inanimate, appears to him in a different light. At first objects and events were valued only for the pleasure or pain which they caused him, but now he measures their value in proportion as they call out the activity and expression of his nature, and thus lead to self-realization and perfection. From the first point of view events are sometimes good, sometimes bad; from the latter point of view they are all equally good. For there is no occasion or circumstance under which the exercise of some virtue and the employment of some faculty are not possible."[42]

Indeed, the optimist who finds ground for hope in every event and traces even in every pain the perfection of the universe, has within himself the means for the realization of his beliefs. For so intimate is the connection between the animal and the spiritual natures that there is a mutual determination between them, and the spiritual states react upon the animal nature as well as the latter upon the former. In other words, the spiritual is not merely acted upon, but exerts the most delicate and powerful influence on the physical. Schiller's medical and poetic lore stand him in good stead here, and furnish him with a multitude of examples and concrete illustrations of his point. Emotional states, such as cheer or mental tranquillity, tend to have a tonic effect upon certain important bodily functions, such as heart action and digestion, while opposite emotional states, such as anxiety, grief and fear, tend to depress and disturb these important functions. The condition, therefore, of greatest momentary mental pleasure is at the same time the condition of the greatest bodily well-being, and optimism and a hopeful mind are more effectual remedies than the pharmacies can furnish."[43]

Aside from these effects, none the less powerful and far-reaching because not directly noticeable, emotions find their external counterpart in facial expression and in gesture, and the most secret movements of the soul are revealed on the exterior of the body. If a passion be often repeated, it will become habitual, and the corresponding physical movements will gradually become engraved upon the exterior of the physical frame, in characters known and read of all men. The good and the beautiful lie close together, so much so that in the delicate interplay of the forces of man's nature they are readily convertible into each other, and the nobility of the spiritual nature is bodied forth in the beautiful form of the physical. "By an admirable law of supreme Wisdom every noble and generous passion beautifies the body, while those that are mean and detestable distort it into animal forms."[44] Thus man has, besides his natural form, acquired features and characteristics; a second face, as it were, not cast in the unchangeable forms of nature, but ever new and changeable under the constant play of the spiritual passions. This acquired physiognomy Schiller calls deuteropathic.

The observations here made are particularly interesting to us because they meet us again in the "fixed" and "movable" beauty in *Anmut und Würde*, and are there elaborately worked out and made the basis of distinctions which are rather important for the understanding of Schiller's moral and æsthetic theory.

(c) The Stage as a Moral Institution

Before closing our consideration of Schiller's early views we must notice briefly two essays of an æsthetico-critical character: *Über das gegenwärtige deutsche Theater*, published in the spring of 1782, and *Die Schaubühne als moralische Anstalt betrachtet*, which comes somewhat more than two years later, in 1784.[45] They are both of interest here, because in them the author approaches definitely the problem of his lifetime, and they show quite unmistakably what function he attributed to objects of æsthetic appreciation at this period of his development.

One cannot but be impressed, in reading these essays, with the more practical and, on the whole, more modern point of view which Schiller here assumes. The narrow walls of the academy had driven his active imagination into all possible and impossible channels, and he took refuge from its stifling atmosphere and trivial artificialities in the idealistic flights of the metaphysical essays and the extravagances of the *Robbers*. But contact with a world of sober reality and practical tasks soon called him back to this mundane sphere, and the experiment, upon the stage, of the *Robbers*[46] gave definite direction to his thought. Traces of metaphysical thought are, indeed, still found here; but even they are utilized to furnish a justification for artistic activity and a basis for æsthetic enjoyment.

The vocation and highest happiness of man, Schiller had said before, is found in the contemplation of the universe, but the full comprehension of it, he had also said, is an infinite task to which the unaided powers of man are, at least in this life, unequal. But what the unaided mind of the ordinary man must relinquish as an impossible task, art may help him to accomplish. For it is just the task of the artist to reproduce the world and human life in miniature, — not any detail of it, for that would serve no better than a fragment of the original, but to reproduce the effect of the whole, by bringing the parts inaccessible to the ordinary eye into view, and thus to prepare the mind to study and appreciate the harmony and symmetry of the great whole.[47] And as man reaches his perfection by the exercise of his functions in the contemplation of the universe, so he is enlightened and perfected by the contemplation of the world in miniature, as represented in the work of the artist.

It would be a mistake, however, to conclude that the Greek ideal of scientific contemplation occupied as prominent a place in these essays as in the earlier writings already considered. While in the passage just alluded to the exercise of the intellectual functions in the contemplation of the universe is still recognized as one of the ends of art, yet it has other functions both more and less serious than the contemplation and admiration of things in general. They are (1) the immediate function of relaxation and æsthetic enjoyment and (2) the ulterior one of moral and intellectual improvement, intellectual improvement being conceived in a more restricted and practical way than on former occasions. Which of these is treated as the more important and which as the subordinate purpose is a question which has given rise to differences of opinion,[48] but which, it seems, hardly admits of discussion. That the pure enjoyment it affords is recognized as one of the ends of art is clear; but that it is not the only one, nor even the highest, is also put beyond question, not only by the explicit statement of more than one passage, but also by the whole tone and tenor of both essays. That the poet is speaking from the point of view of the statesman, when enlarging upon the possibilities of the stage as an instrument of education and of moral improvement, is, of course, true; but that he himself adopted this standpoint, and that he looked upon the natural bent of man for relaxation and æsthetic enjoyment as an invaluable means to be used for higher ends, he states almost in so many words. After referring to the immediate effect of art in inducing the harmonious activity of the various powers of man's nature, thus restoring the integrity which has been disrupted by the one-sided employments and preoccupations of life, he immediately adds: "But since it should be the first object of a wise statesman to select the higher of two effects, he will not be content with simply disarming the inclinations of his people; he will, if possible, use them as instruments for higher uses, and endeavor to convert them into sources of happiness. To this end he has selected the stage as the best means of opening an endless sphere to the spirit craving activity, and of exercising every power of the soul without straining any, and combining the cultivation of the understanding and the heart with the noblest entertainment."

The relation which the stage sustains to the other moral institutions, religion and law, is indicated in clear and persuasive language, and the discussion shows the finest insight into moral questions. The inadequacy and uncertainty of political laws, which render religion necessary, likewise determine the moral influence of the stage. Laws impose only negative duties; religion enjoins positive acts. Laws control only the outward manifestations of the will; religion extends her jurisdiction to the heart.

But can religion achieve the whole of human culture? The very thing which gives religion its power also imposes limitations upon it. The appeal of religion is through the images of sense; but the pictures of religion are only pictures of the fancy, its problems are without solution, its phantoms of terror and its allurements act only from a distance. Not so with the stage. Here, too, you have life pictured in the vivid images of sense; but they are images which stand for ever-present realities. Here vice and virtue, happiness and misery, wisdom and folly, pass before the view with all their natural and inevitable issues and consequences, and the beauty of virtue and the hideousness of vice are fully displayed. When morality is no longer taught, religion no longer believed in, and laws have ceased to exist, Medea and Macbeth will still exert a powerful influence upon the hearts of men.

The sphere of the stage is much wider than that of religion and justice. Where these deem it beneath their dignity to go the stage still continues to work for culture. In jest and satire it possesses more powerful weapons than the tortures of law or the terrors of conscience. A thousand vices unnoticed by human justice are punished by the stage, and a thousand virtues which the law does not regard are recognized and recommended.

The stage is a school of practical wisdom and civic duty. It teaches the workings of fate and fortune; it makes us sympathize with and judge leniently the unfortunate, and it spreads the spirit of religious tolerance. It might be employed to correct errors and blunders in education, and if the proper subjects were chosen, it could be used as an instrument to attain national solidarity. "If a national stage should be inaugurated, the Germans might become a nation."[49]

It is in the sentence just quoted that the explanation of the somewhat inflated estimate of the moral possibilities of the stage, in the later of the two essays, must be sought. Schiller had just been appointed theatre poet at Mannheim, and Lessing's idea of a national stage was seriously occupying him. He had also been honored with membership in the Electoral German Society, and it was before a public session of this body that the essay was first read. It is therefore a matter of no great surprise that this view of the stage as an instrument of moral and civic education should have been developed in this one-sided fashion, and its more purely æsthetic function have been somewhat neglected. That he at this time recognized the independent value of art may be pretty safely assumed, but cannot be definitely proved from his writings. At any rate, the characterization of the æsthetic condition as a *state of repose*, a harmony into which the tension due to a one-sided activity of our sensuous or our spiritual nature is resolved, is sufficiently noteworthy. It is the formulation of the æsthetic condition in the *Æsthetic Letters*, at the time of his greatest speculative activity.

It will be well to bring together some of the main results reached in the consideration of Schiller's early philosophical writings, and to recall briefly the ideas which, in a developed and a more explicit way, meet us again in the later stages of the poet's development. (1) The earliest philosophical writings of Schiller are in the spirit of the German Illumination, in which elements of the Leibniz-Wolffian philosophy and of the Scottish school are variously combined and loosely held together. The influence of Shaftesbury,[50] Hutcheson, and the eclectic Ferguson, is unmistakable. The decided Aristotelian coloring of some of Schiller's moral reflections is due to Garve, the translator of Ferguson's *Moral Philosophy,* an appreciative student, also, and translator of ancient ethical literature. Haller also exerted considerable influence over Schiller, not only on his physiological studies, but also on the psychophysical views developed in the academic dissertations. (2) A deeply moral and human interest manifests itself throughout the early writings. The nature of virtue, the vocation and end of the moral agent — these are the questions which occupy Schiller's most serious attention. And while in the discussion of the latter question the emphasis is shifted somewhat from the end as pleasure or perfection to the end as activity of man's powers, this must not be interpreted to mean that Schiller abandoned the eudæmonistic view of ethics, which, in a moderate form, he always adhered to. As in the earlier period of Greek speculation, virtue and self-interest were not conceived as opposed to each other in the current moral philosophy, but pleasurable feeling was conceived as a natural and necessary consequence of the exercise of wisdom or virtue, and as such held to be a constituent element of the good. (3) Another striking feature of the writings considered is the thoroughgoing dualism between the natural and the spiritual, and more particularly, of the sensuous and rational elements in man's nature. His defence of the affective life, the feelings, instincts and impulses, and his attempt at a mediation between the so-called lower and higher natures, first by means of a metaphysical intermediate agent, later by means of art, foreshadow the whole course of his future thinking. (4) Interesting, too, in view of future ethical and æsthetic theory, in view, also, of the more distinctly literary work of the "poet of liberty," is his attitude on the subject of the freedom of the will, a subject which was always an attractive one for the young philosopher, and which is discussed with more than ordinary originality and acumen in the Master's Dissertation. How much the subject occupied his thought during the last year in the academy is shown by the fact that the subject *Freedom and Morality* was contemplated for his dissertation, and actually offered along with the more comprehensive subject eventually chosen.[51] (5) In this connection may be recalled the view of the dynamic character of the individual. As the perfection of the monad consists, according to Leibniz, in the free development of its active powers, so the true being of the individual and his perfection consist, according to Schiller, in the activity of all his powers in due proportion. With this view is closely connected (6) the theory of evolution which, in its broadest aspect, was already clearly conceived and unhesitatingly accepted in the Master's Dissertation. (7) Of interest to the student of Schiller's æsthetic theory, especially, is the view clearly indicated, though only scantily discussed, of the physiology of the senses. The sense organs appear not as mere channels or conductors through which impressions are carried to the mind, as in the naïve view of English Empiricism, but rather as transforming powers by which the physical processes of the external world are modified, "so that they may be able to awaken ideas within us." Here the influence of Leibniz's theory of presentation is clearly evident.[52] (8) Intimately connected with the view of the necessary relation of the affective life and human welfare, and involved as a corollary, is the view of the significance, in human life, of the pleasing, *i. e.*, of æsthetic objects. Approaches to this, the fundamental problem of the period of the *Artists* and of the *Letters on the Æsthetic Education of the*

Human Race, are found not only in the metaphysical essays of the Academy, but the problem is definitely faced and explicitly, though somewhat one-sidedly, discussed in the dramaturgical essays of the first period.

CHAPTER IV

AWAKENING

The Philosophical Letters and Related Poems

THE value of the *Philosophical Letters* has been variously estimated. Nevinson [53] sees in them only "empty speculations" and "vapid, unprofitable musings," while Hoffmeister [54] can speak of them only in words of the most extravagant praise, finding in them a depth and truth of ideas, a sanity of judgment, a purity of feeling, and a beauty of expression unsurpassed in German literature. As is almost always the case, the truth will be found somewhere between the extreme opinions. While the *Letters* do not represent the cautious and painstaking thought of a mature and systematic mind, they do reveal a mind of unusual intelligence and restless striving, and a temperament of the deepest seriousness. But whatever the intrinsic value of the *Letters* as philosophic literature may be, their value to the student of the growth of Schiller's reflective life is unquestioned, and it is for their biographical value that they must be somewhat closely examined. For it is here, and notably in the two poems published about the same time, though perhaps already written during the second Mannheim period,[55] the *Freigeisterei der Leidenschaft* and *Resignation*, that the traditional views so enthusiastically espoused in the writings already discussed begin to relax their hold upon Schiller, and the old landmarks are permanently removed from their places. While the two poems represent a decided change of front in his moral *Weltanschauung*, the *Philosophical Letters* show us the dissolution of his metaphysics. The right of every man to a just share of happiness had always been unquestioned by Schiller, and the boundless optimism of his first writings never conceived of a state in which the rewards of happiness were not along the path of virtue.[56] The right to happiness is still unqualifiedly asserted in the lyrics mentioned, but the opposition of virtue and pleasure, of duty and inclination, rises into sharp prominence. Which side Schiller takes in the conflict he does not leave us in doubt:

"No, I this conflict will no longer wage
The conflict duty claims — the giant task —
Thy spells, O Virtue, never can assuage
The heart's wild fire — this offering do not ask!

"True, I have sworn — a solemn vow have sworn
That I myself will curb the self within;
Yet take thy wreath, no more it shall be worn —
Take back thy wreath and leave me free to sin."[57]

The close of the poem, in which Schiller roundly denounces a God who takes pleasure in our tears and bloody renunciation, who has led the path to heaven across the depths of hell, has, notwithstanding the explanation which Schiller himself appended to the poem, been severely criticized. It would hardly be fair, after what Schiller has said, to take the poem as a " philosophical system " or a calm confession of faith once for all delivered. But after all is said, it remains that the poet was at the time of the writing keenly alive to the profound breach between virtue, conventional or other, and inclination, between " the law of the flesh and the law of the spirit."

The same breach between virtue and welfare meets us again in the lyric, *Resignation*, beginning with the well-known lines:

" I, too, was born in fair Arcadia's land.
To me did nature too
Swear at my cradle joys on every hand;
I, too, was born in fair Arcadia's land,
But clouds of tears eclipsed the springtide's blue."

Just what the meaning of this perplexing poem is has been often discussed, without any particularly enlightening result. One thing, however, is pretty certain, that virtue and happiness, in the early essays always thought of as inseparable from each other, are here rather sharply opposed, if not conceived as absolutely incompatible elements in the moral life; and this is significant for Schiller's development from the purely eudæmonistic standpoint of his earlier writings to the more rigoristic conception of the Kantian period. The theistic attitude has given way to a decidedly skeptical view, and the implicit trust in the harmony and rationality of the universe, so characteristic of the earliest period of the poet's reflection, is decidedly shaken. Nor is the hope of a future existence in which the present imperfect order is to be rectified left to him:

> "Giv'st thou sure joy for hope that disappears
> Into corrupted mold?
> Death has been silent for six thousand years;
> Nor from the grave one corpse to living ears
> Of the Requiter told."

Nature is divided against herself; life is full of problems and conflicts without solution or issue, and "hope disappears into corrupted mold."

The *Philosophical Letters* interest us not only because we have in them the restatement of the early metaphysical views of Schiller, and his comment upon them from the point of view of the present transition period, but also some important information regarding the influences which destroyed "the dreams," as he somewhere calls them, "of his imagination." The letters purport to be the correspondence between

Schiller and Körner, and some of them were actually passed between the two men during the time of their most intimate intercourse, between September, 1785, and April, 1786.

The general events of Schiller's life between the time of the school-days and the present period, and the incidents which led to the remarkable friendship between Schiller and Körner, are fairly well known, but may be briefly recalled here in view of the influence which the external circumstances of his life had upon the susceptible mind of Schiller, and in view, particularly, of the far-reaching influence of Körner upon his development at this time. For with his inner development the varied fortunes and personal relations of Schiller's early life had, doubtless, not a little to do, as has often been pointed out by his biographers. We have already seen in the discussion of the dramaturgical essays the sobering effect which contact with the world had upon him. In them we find him occupying himself with the problems confronting him in his professional career to the almost total neglect of the favorite metaphysical views of only a few years before, though he felt no necessity or had no occasion to express any change of attitude regarding what he had considered the fundamental verities of life. But the fortunes of his life continued to be such as to make a gradual and even development of his inner life extremely improbable. His life continued one of sharp and steady conflict, a conflict between aspiration and fact, between his vocation and his lot, between the desire for independent activity and the barriers of irrational necessity, between his genius, in short, and the limitations of his life.

Schiller's engagement as theatre-poet at Mannheim was only for one year, and terminated August, 1784, setting him adrift again. *Fiesko* and *Kabale und Liebe* had been produced in the winter and spring of that year, the former a failure which, however, the success of the latter somewhat retrieved. Whatever reputation Schiller enjoyed with certain classes of the people, it is evident that their enthusiasm was little shared by those upon whose purses and influence the successes and failures of the literary world so largely depend. Involved in financial embarrassment, and some dangerous "friendships," so common at the time, with sundry female admirers, with no definite prospects or plans for the future and no friends whose services extended beyond sympathy and good wishes, he resolved to avail himself of an offer which had come to him some months before, and which was destined to mark a turning-point in his career. A letter had been received by him, June, 1784, from a circle of friends and admirers in Leipzig, chief of whom was Christian Gottfried Körner, father of the illustrious poet of the War of Liberation, in which they expressed the highest admiration for Schiller's genius, at the same time enclosing crayon portraits of his admirers. Though Schiller did not reply to the letter until December, a steady correspondence was then begun which finally resulted in Schiller's leaving Mannheim to join his friends in Leipzig, where he arrived April 17th, 1785.

The relation that existed between Schiller and Körner has been well characterized by Professor Royce: "His (Körner's) place in Schiller's early development was one of quiet and kindly opposition. When Schiller is in despair, Körner encourages him. When Schiller jumps at conclusions, Körner invites him to study philosophy, and trust more to his understanding. When Schiller plunges into hard study, Körner reminds him of his vocation as a poet. And so throughout — with a curious mingling of affection, criticism, reverence, advice — Körner gives his great friend just the stay the perplexed soul needed."[58] It was Körner, himself an ardent Kantian from the beginning, by whom Schiller was first introduced to the Kantian philosophy, and it is in these *Letters* that the influence of Kantian ideas first makes itself clearly felt.

It is a matter of some importance for our present purpose to determine as accurately as possible the authorship, and, particularly, the dates of composition of the different parts of the letters, a question which is involved in some obscurity, and on which, although it has been exhaustively studied, there has existed considerable diversity of opinion. That the bulk of the five letters were written in the winter of 1785-6, during the time of the first acquaintance between Schiller and Körner, and that they are the realization of a plan for a philosophical romance in the form of letters conceived several years before, is certain. That Körner had a part in writing the *Raphael* letters is also beyond question, especially in the case of the last letter of April 4th, 1788, to which Körner's initial is affixed, and to which Schiller replied in his own name in a letter elsewhere published.[59] It is the date of the fourth letter, which contains the so-called *Theosophy of Julius*, that has been the source of considerable difficulty to literary critics. According to Tomaschek, the *Theosophy of Julius* was written during the Stuttgart period, or in 1781 at the latest, when the *Philosophical Romance in Letters between Julius and Raphael* was projected, while Schiller's comments upon it, about four pages in all, preceding and following it, were written at this time, that is, in the winter or spring, perhaps, of 1786. Hoffmeister, Minor and others are also of the opinion that the principal part, at least, of the *Theosophy* is an interpolation, and was written toward the end of the academic period. This opinion, however, is not shared by Kuno Fischer, who has argued his case with a brilliancy and breadth of view that makes his conclusion very attractive, if not well-nigh inevitable. He points out [60] close correspondences between certain paragraphs of the *Theosophy* and later poems, between the paragraphs *Love* and *Sacrifice*, particularly, and the poem *Resignation*, just noticed, and the characterization of the Marquis Posa in *Don Carlos*, both of which productions belong, of course, to the present period. It is easy, however, to conclude too much from these resemblances, which are not so close and fundamental but that they might have occurred between writings considerably separated from each other in time and spirit. At any rate, the similarities between the *Theosophy* and *Resignation* and *Don Carlos* are no greater than the similarities between the *Theosophy* and the writings of the Stuttgart period, the Master's Dissertation, the poem *Die Freundschaft* and other poems of the *Anthology*, quotations from which actually appear in this part of the *Philosophical Letters*. Schiller's own testimony, of course, is well known and has often been quoted. "I have been looking over my papers this morning," he says in the opening lines of the fourth letter, "and I find a lost essay, sketched in those happy hours of my proud enthusiasm. But how different everything seems to me now," etc. The view, therefore, which on the whole commends itself as the right one is that the *Theosophy of Julius* was written at a considerably earlier time than the remainder of the *Philosophical Letters*, and that it belongs chronologically to the group of writings already dealt with under the title, *Early Views*. This does not, of course, exclude the possibility that portions of the manuscript were subjected to revision before it was incorporated in the body of the *Philosophical Letters*, to which it was supposed to be a complete contrast.[61]

It will not be necessary here to give a résumé of the contents of the *Theosophy of Julius*, the leading ideas of which, when disentangled from their elaborate rhetorical dress, are in the main those that we found in the Master's Dissertation. It is the comments which Schiller makes upon these ideas in the remaining parts of the *Letters* that interest us, and it is upon these that our attention must be mainly directed. It is significant to notice, at the outset, that Julius speaks of his former views as views to which he was led by his heart and his imagination, and that he contrasts them with the rational or reflective attitude to which he was led by his friend, Raphael. "I felt and was happy. Raphael has taught me to think, and I am on the way to regret that I was ever created." "You have robbed me of the faith that gave me peace. You have taught me to despise where I prayed before. A thousand things were venerable in my sight, till your dismal wisdom stripped off the veil from them." The world is a divine work of art, he had said, in the contemplation and imitation of which man finds his highest vocation and perfection, and the view had afforded satisfaction and stimulus to his artist's imagination. But Raphael heartlessly suggests that the world is a rather large object for the human mind to aim at and completely interpret, but that such bold attempts are natural enough at certain stages in the development of the individual or racial mind. "It was most natural that your philosophical career began as with the human race in general. The object on which man's spirit of inquiry first attempted its strength was, at all times, the universe. Hypotheses regarding the origin of the world and the connection of its parts had occupied the greatest thinkers for ages, when Socrates called down the philosophy of his time from heaven to earth."

Of all the propositions of Julius he can least agree with the one which assumes that the highest destiny of man is to detect the spirit of the divine Artist in the work of creation, and he points out an important distinction between the universe and the work of a human artist. The work of a human artist is the pure expression of an ideal. He governs despotically the inanimate matter which he uses to body forth his ideas. "But in the divine work of art the individuality and worth of each one of its parts is respected, and the respect with which the divine Architect honors every germ of energy, even in the lowliest creature, glorifies him just as much as the harmony of the immeasurable whole. *Life* and *freedom* in every part characterize the divine creation, and it is nowhere more sublime than where it seems to have departed most widely from its ideal." [62]

The dynamic and animistic view of nature of Leibniz and Herder could hardly have found a clearer expression than in this sentence. The belief in the purposiveness of creation, so firmly adhered to in the earlier writings, also fails to stand the test of cold reflection. Means and ends, the Prince declares in the *Geisterseher*, which was written later but still belongs to this period, are merely human conceptions, and cannot be applied beyond the sphere of our activity. If a crystal were endowed with consciousness, it would doubtless see in crystallization the end and realization of the world plan. In other words, teleology is not an objective principle of explanation, like physical causality, but only a subjective principle of reflection, and applicable, therefore, only within the limited sphere of human activity.

The one idea, indeed, that runs throughout the whole of the *Philosophical Letters*, and for that matter through all the writings of this period, is the idea of the relativity and limitation of human desire and knowledge. "All things in heaven and earth have no value, no estimation, except that which my reason grants them," exclaims Julius in the first intoxication of his new view. "But unhappy contradiction of nature," he immediately adds, "this free and soaring spirit is joined to the rigid, mechanical clockwork of a mortal body, bound up with its little necessities, yoked to its miserable fate — this God is banished into a world of worms." [63] Man cannot think of two ideas at one time. For one enjoyment he must resign all others; two unlimited desires are too great for his little heart. "Human nature has its proper bounds," he says in the closing remarks of the fourth letter, "and so also has the individual." The human mind surveys the supersensible by means of the sensible, and mathematics applies its conclusions to the mystery of the superhuman. But this knowledge of the supersensible world is forever beyond the possibility of verification: "No traveler has returned from that land to relate his discovery."[64]

The reader acquainted with the philosophical writings of Kant cannot but have noticed the striking similarity between the ideas here set forth and the leading principles of the Critical Philosophy. And when Schiller says that "our purest ideas are by no means images of things, but only their signs or symbols," that "truth is no property of the symbols, but of the conclusion; it is not the likeness of the sign with the thing signified, of the conception with the object, but the agreement of this conception with the laws of thought;" when he refers to the self-deception which men practise when they "dissect a conception into the separate elements out of which it was first compounded by an act of caprice," and imagine they have discovered new truths, or when he speaks of the "endemic forms" of our thought, we can have little doubt from what quarters the influence came that destroyed the dreams of his imagination, and called down his philosophy from heaven to earth. For it was one of the principal problems of the Kantian philosophy, and its lasting merit, to have set the proper limits to speculative inquiry, limits beyond which reason could not go without landing in self-contradiction.

That Schiller had not read the *Critique of Pure Reason* at this time is shown conclusively by a letter to Körner, written at Weimar, April 15th, 1788. In view of the close connection it has with the *Philosophical Letters*, and in view of the valuable remarks it contains on Schiller's philosophical reading, it will be interesting to quote from it at some length. "Your letter to Julius (the last of the *Philosophical Letters*) was a complete surprise. I did not suspect that you were busy, and busy for me! It contains some bright ideas as to how even an active and independent mind can bear the yoke of the opinion of others, and how it is that such a mind, if delivered from this yoke, will take just this course. . . . That my Julius made his first attempt on the universe, is perhaps due to my peculiar position; it is owing to my having studied almost no other philosophy, and to my not having become acquainted with any other by chance. From the few philosophical works I have read, I always appropriated that which appealed to my poetic temperament and lent itself to poetic treatment. It was thus that this subject which opened so rich a field for the imagination, became my favorite study. Your remarks on the juggling tricks of reason whereby to escape the truth in order to save a system I find very excellent; they have thrown light on my own problems. I am very much mistaken if your innocent remarks on the dry investigations on human cognition and the humiliating limits of human reason are not a distant threat with — the study of Kant. I'll wager you will bring him up again. I know the wolf by his howl. Well, I believe that you are entirely right; but it still goes against the grain with me to enter upon this subject." [65]

Just at what time Schiller took up the study of Kant, with what motives, and to what extent he read the writings of the Critical Philosophy, are questions which we reserve for a separate chapter. That he would read them is only what we should have expected of an active and earnest mind, which must almost inevitably have been plunged into a period of skepticism, but which nevertheless could not permanently rest in it. Hoffmeister has called the *Philosophical Letters* a history of philosophy reproduced in the individual, and the comparison which Körner suggests between the course of Schiller's early development and the history of early Greek philosophy will be found not inapt by one acquainted with this period of human thought. Dogmatism, skepticism, criticism, — these are the stages through which reflective thought has more than once passed. The earliest period of Greek philosophy was characterized by its interest in the physical universe; philosophy was cosmo-centric and dogmatic. This period was followed by one of skepticism, inaugurated by the Sophists, in which by a subtle, subjective dialectic all that had been objectively established in the way of custom, religious belief and law was undermined. Almost immediately succeeding this skeptical and relativistic period begins that splendid era of Greek philosophy with which the names of Socrates, Plato and Aristotle are so intimately associated, — an era of criticism and many-sided scientific activity, with which the great period of European thought in the nineteenth century may be broadly compared.

The influence that any one reformer exercises on his time, it is safe to say, is almost always overestimated, owing to the fact that too exclusive attention is paid by the historian to the particular man or system with whose cause or doctrine he has identified his interests. But it will be conceded by all that when one comes to estimate the relative influence of different individuals in shaping the philosophy, and the thought in general, of the nineteenth century, the work of Kant in defining the conditions and limits of knowledge must be pronounced a lasting achievement, and accorded an honorable place, and that even his contributions to the sciences of ethics and æsthetics, whatever one may think of their present value, must be granted a large historical significance. Schiller was destined to be one of the first to be caught up by the wave of enthusiasm for the Kantian philosophy which swept the land, and the part he played in the development of those very sciences to which Kant gave a strong impetus, but which his natural limitations, and what seems to us an unreasonable adherence to certain metaphysical principles, kept him from developing to their fullest extent, — the part which Schiller played in the broadening and advancing of the sciences of ethics and æsthetics, has perhaps not been sufficiently recognized: and this not because of the slight significance of his scientific writings, but because these are overshadowed, in the popular consciousness, by that incomparable line of dramatic writings the names of which have become household words wherever the influence of German letters has extended. Schiller is known not as the author of *Anmut und Würde* and the *Æsthetic Letters*, but as the author of *Tell* and *Wallenstein.* Precisely what was the part he played in the broadening, as we have called it, and the advance upon the Kantian principles, we must inquire presently.

CHAPTER V

THE STUDY OF KANT

That Schiller had some acquaintance with the Kantian philosophy perhaps as early as 1786, that is, during his Dresden period, has been seen from the decidedly Kantian coloring of some of the passages in the *Philosophical Letters;* but that his acquaintance with it was not very intimate or extensive is also seen, not only from the vagueness and looseness with which Kantian principles are employed, but from the direct statements of Schiller himself, one of which has already been quoted at some length. What knowledge of the Kantian writings he possessed he had perhaps gleaned mostly from the long and earnest conversations with Körner, which he is reported to have had, and from the regular correspondence with his friend, whose letters and other writings show him to have been a man of philosophical temperament and varied interests, though the variety of his interests and the somewhat desultory character of his literary efforts kept him from going far beyond the stage of dilettantism in any line. The first writings of Kant which Schiller actually read, and the only ones before 1791, so far as there is any record, were the two small treatises *Idee zu einer allgemeinen Geschichte in weltbürgerlicher Absicht* and *Muthmasslicher Anfang der Menschengeschichte*, both published in the Berlin *Monatsschrift*. "Reinhold's lectures," he writes to Körner August 29th, 1787, after a visit to Jena, "commence in October; they include Kant's Philosophy and the Fine Arts. In comparison to Reinhold, you are an enemy of Kant's: he maintains that a hundred years hence Kant's reputation will be unbounded. But I must avow that he spoke of him with great judgment, and has already induced me to commence reading Kant's small treatises in the *Berlin Monthly Review*, amongst which his idea of a universal history gave me great satisfaction. That I shall read Kant, and perhaps study his works, is, I see, more than probable. Reinhold told me that Kant was about to publish a treatise on Practical Reason, or on the Will; and afterwards a Treatise on Taste. Rejoice, then, beforehand." [66]

When Schiller went to Jena, May, 1789, to assume his duties as professor "extraordinary" of history, to which he had been appointed mainly through Goethe's influence, he found himself in a very nest of Kantians, and heard the Kantian principles extolled until, as he says, he was nearly surfeited with them (*zum Satt-werden preisen*). Jena was known at this time as the second home of the Kantian philosophy, and its fame was attracting students from all parts of Germany and the northern countries, many of whom were either already enthusiastic adherents of the Kantian philosophy, or were filled with curiosity to know more about the destructive and novel theories which, as they were told, must produce a revolution in philosophy. That Schiller was on very intimate terms with the teaching force of the University does not appear from his correspondence; indeed, the enthusiasm which the students displayed on Schiller's arrival was by no means shared by his colleagues, some of whom were only glad enough of an opportunity to humiliate him.

Schiller's impression of Reinhold, the apostle, as he was called, of the new philosophical gospel, was never very favorable, and the interesting description Schiller gives of his character and personality shows the deep temperamental differences existing between the two men. "You must not, however, conclude from this description," he writes to Körner, "that Reinhold and I are friends, or will become so. Reinhold can never become my friend, nor I his, although he fancies so. His reason is cold, deep and clear-sighted — mine is not, nor can I appreciate him; but his imagination is poor and circumscribed, and his mind is narrower than mine. . . . His sentiments are scraped together and fall heavily. . . . His ideas of moral virtues are more timid than mine, and his effeminacy at times approaches cowardice. He never could be capable of great virtues, or great crimes, either in imagination or in reality, and that is bad. I can be the friend of no man who is not capable of one or the other, or both."[67]

It is not probable that a man so unattractive to Schiller could exert a great influence over the poet, who was busy fourteen hours a day preparing lectures for students on a subject about which, as he frankly confesses, "many of them would probably know more than the professor." But it was inevitable that a mind so sensitive to everything that went on about him, and so eager to appropriate anything which might set him to rights on problems in which he felt a perennial interest, would have been infected with the Kantian enthusiasm everywhere manifested.[68] For it would be an error to conclude from some of his statements that he was in any way antagonistic to the new philosophy. The apparent indifference with which he repeatedly speaks of it would be explained by the conjecture that he was less interested in the problems of epistemology of the first Critique, than in the treatises on Taste and Morals which had been promised, and which Schiller hailed with joy, — a conjecture which is made probable by the general tenor of his interests, as we have known them, and which is confirmed by the fact that he actually read only the *Critique of Judgment* and the utterances of Kant on the subjects of Morality. The intense ethical fervor of Schiller's nature attached itself only too readily to a system whose ruggedness and noble sweep came as a genuine relief to minds weary of the prolix pedantry of the reigning philosophy and the shallow eudæmonism so prevalent at the end of the eighteenth century. The boudoir philosophy and the insipid moralizings of the Enlightenment must have appeared in strange contrast, to all healthy minds, to the impressive utterances of Kant, the very difficulties and the cumbrous terminology of whose writings exercised a strange fascination over the younger generation of that period. Schiller himself, as Nevinson says, " though not a philosopher, had a natural inclination to things abstract, intangible and remote; nor did he require that stimulus of the rewards that even an unphilosophic mind may gain from the study of Kant — delight in the sense of the power and solidity of a supreme intellect, in the passages of stern eloquence where the very strength of thought endues the rugged expression with grandeur, and in the fervor of a living purpose which inspires and kindles the whole." [69]

Schiller accordingly needed only an opportunity to devote himself in earnest to the study of the Kantian philosophy. This opportunity came to him in March, 1791, when his literary labors had been interrupted by the first attack of a serious illness, the effects of which he never outgrew, and which eventually brought on his premature death. Through the influence of the Danish poet, Jens Baggesen, Frederick Christian, the Prince of Schleswig-Holstein Augustenburg, and Count Schimmelmann, presented Schiller with the handsome gift of a thousand thalers annually for three years, to free him from want and to make possible his recovery. The joy Schiller experienced may be best conveyed by quoting his letter to Körner: ". . . What I have longed for so intensely during my whole life, is now to be fulfilled. I have got rid of every care and every anxiety for a long period, perhaps forever. I have at last attained the long coveted independence of spirit. I have the immediate prospect of arranging my affairs, and paying off all my debts, and, freed from any solicitude about the means of existence, I can now live entirely in accordance with the impulses of my mind. I have at last leisure to concentrate my thoughts, and to toil for eternity."

The first book of Kant's to which he devoted himself was the *Critique of Judgment,* which had just been published, in the spring of 1790. "You cannot guess," he wrote to Körner, March 5th, 1791, "what I am reading and studying. Nothing worse than Kant. His *Critique of Judgment*, which I have bought for myself, is carrying me away by its pregnant and illuminating contents, and has inspired me with the greatest desire to work myself more and more into his philosophy. . . . I do not imagine that Kant will be such an insurmountable obstacle, and I shall doubtless study him still more carefully."

He had intended to continue his lectures on æsthetics during the winter of the same year, and intended to master the Kantian æsthetics preparatory to them. The lectures, however, were postponed until the winter of 1792-3, and he had ample opportunity, in the meantime, to busy himself with his favorite pursuit. "I am now hard at work at Kant's philosophy," he writes to Körner, January 1st, 1792, "and I wish I could have a discussion with you every evening on the subject. I am fully determined not to lay it down until I have thoroughly mastered it, even if it should take me three years to do so."

Nor was his interest confined to the Kantian philosophy. He would like, he adds, to study

Locke, Hume and Leibniz at the same time, and inquires about a good translation of Locke. He would undertake one himself, if he were sufficiently master of the English language. Again in May he writes that he is busy with the *Thirty Years' War*, and in studying Kant's *Critique of Judgment* preparatory to the *Æsthetic Letters*, which, it appears, he had planned as early as this. He intends also to read Baumgarten first, he says, and hopes Körner will "see if anything can be done with Sulzer."

In this same letter occurs a passage which has been quoted more than once to show the baneful effect which the study of philosophy is supposed to have had upon the mind of Schiller, who fell "only too easily," we are told, "into all the tricks of the metaphysical trade." "I feel," says Schiller, "that ever since I have acted according to laid-down rules, I have lost that boldness and living fire I formerly possessed. I now see what I create and form. I watch the progress of the fruits of inspiration; and my imagination is less free, since it is aware that it is watched." Schiller was an artistic mind and had splendid natural endowments, everyone will grant; but he was too much of an artist, and he had too much natural endowment, to imagine for a moment that the knowledge of the principles one employs in artistic creation, provided it goes far enough, will detract from the value of the artistic product, or that insight is incompatible with inspiration. "For practice' sake," says Schiller, "I like a philosophical discussion on theories, and criticism must now remedy what it has spoiled, — for it has spoiled me. . . . When I have succeeded in making the laws laid down by art second nature, in like manner as education makes the polished man, imagination will then reassert its former freedom, and will prescribe its own limits." [70] It will be cheerfully granted by all literary critics that some of the "boldness and living fire" which Schiller formerly possessed and which he lost could very well have been dispensed with, and some of the productions of the pre-critical period been none the worse for it. Carlyle puts the case admirably: "Excellence," he says, "not ease of composition, is the thing to be desired; and in a mind like Schiller's, so full of energy, of images and thoughts and creative power, the more sedulous practice of selection was little likely to be detrimental." [71]

It is of course idle to speculate on what might or might not have been if the conditions had been different from what they were, and it may be that Schiller's work might have excelled in artistic finish and extent anything that he actually did, if he had never given serious study to the principles, philosophic or what not, according to which artistic production proceeds. It remains that the permanent work of Schiller's life was accomplished after, and not before, his study of philosophy, and the splendid achievements of the years immediately succeeding the Kantian period furnish a *prima facie* justification of all the means of development and self-improvement which he so assiduously employed: the study of history, of Greek literature, and of philosophy. Nothing could be more misleading than the suggestion that Schiller's philosophy and his poetry were two things apart. From the *Odes to Laura* through the various productions of his *Ideendichtung* and the dramas of his last period, the poetic and reflective elements are most intimately interwoven; indeed, it is inconceivable how a poet so profoundly ethical as Schiller could keep his art and his philosophy permanently separate. In the *Ideendichtung* philosophical problems are consciously made the objects of poetic treatment, and some of the poems present a perfection of form hardly paralleled in the language. Of course it is easy to say that such poetry is not poetry in the true sense of the term; but that is only the worse for poetry "in the true sense of the term." To treat intellectual or moral problems in such a way as to give the most exquisite pleasure to cultivated minds is not to overstep the limits of art, but to extend them.

In thus defending Schiller's study of philosophy it is not meant to justify the pedantry and artificiality with which philosophy in general and Kant in particular have so often been charged. That there is useless machinery in Kant's system is a fact too notorious to be insisted on: it would have been an extraordinary thing if philosophy alone had escaped the vagueness which enveloped and the pedantry which weighed down all the rest of the sciences.

Schiller returned again and again to his philosophical studies. On October 15th he speaks of studying the *Critique of Judgment* again, and expresses his determination not to rest until he has "mastered it, and made something of it." By December he had reached some positive results. His study of æsthetics has thrown much light upon the nature of the beautiful, he writes, and he believes that he has discovered "the objective idea of the beautiful which is qualified, *eo ipso*, to be the objective principle upon which taste is founded, and about which Kant tormented his brain without success."[72] The quotation is significant: for it is this point, that is, the establishment of the objective character of the beautiful, about which much of the interest of his æsthetic writings turns, and which marks the departure from, and the advance upon, the Kantian theory of æsthetics. To the discussion of the æsthetic theory proper we shall give some incidental attention in connection with a group of writings mainly ethical in interest, which appear among the first results of the Kantian studies, — the essays *Über den Grund des Vergnügens an tragischen Gegenständen*, *Über die tragische Kunst*, and, as representing a more independent attitude toward the Kantian morality, the essay *Anmut und Würde* and the group of minor writings related to it in content and general aim.

That Schiller read the *Critique of Practical Reason* perhaps as early as 1791 is asserted by several authorities,[73] and is made probable by the influence the leading ideas of this work exercised upon the writings immediately following this time, though I have not been able to find conclusive evidence regarding the matter among Schiller's own utterances. Whether or not Schiller ever read the *Critique of Pure Reason* appears doubtful, but there is no conclusive evidence one way or the other. That Schiller intended making a study of the work is shown by the fact that he actually ordered it, as his letter to the book-dealer Crusius of December 16th, 1791, shows; and the fact that he expresses a desire to study Locke, Hume and Leibniz in the letter of January 1st, 1792, noticed above, shows that he did not intend to confine himself to those parts of Kant's philosophy which were of most immediate interest to him in his practical work in writing and lecturing, but was determined to acquaint himself with the whole theoretical groundwork of the Critical Philosophy. The circumstance, however, that he never refers to his study of the first *Critique* and the philosophy out of which it grew, though he was always very communicative about his work, makes it pretty safe to say that the press of work and his absorbing interest in the theory of æsthetics never allowed him to make much headway in the study of the more theoretical parts of the Critical writings.

CHAPTER VI

FIRST FRUITS

The Essays on the Tragic

To call the two essays on the tragic, to be discussed under this head, the first results or first fruits of the study of Kant, as has been done, perhaps requires some explanation. The large amount of material in them which is apparently uninfluenced by the Kantian æsthetics may perhaps puzzle those who had expected a close adhesion to, or an almost verbal repetition of, the Kantian ideas, such as one is more than likely to expect from the description given of the essays by most of the writers who have made allusion to them. The somewhat heterogeneous character and the wavering tone actually found in the writings in question is completely explained by the circumstances of their composition. Most of the material contained in them was already brought together for the lectures on æsthetics given by Schiller during the summer of 1790. Whatever knowledge he may have possessed of the literature on æsthetics at that time, we have his word for it that he did not depend upon it in the elaboration of his lectures, and there is no reason to believe that he was to any appreciable extent influenced by the *Critique of Judgment*, although this had already appeared in the spring of the same year. He is giving a *publicum* on the tragic, he writes to Körner, May 16th, 1790; "but do not imagine," he adds, "that I am consulting a single authority. I am making this æsthetic myself, and it is none the worse for that either, according to my opinion."[74] "My theory of tragedy," he says again June 18th, "to which I devote one day each week, is a great source of pleasure to me. Of course I get along slowly, as I do not use a single book, but rely entirely upon my past experience and examples from tragic compositions." It is Schiller's own theory of tragedy, therefore, precipitated from a rather intimate and varied acquaintance with tragic literature, and from an unusually successful experience of ten years as a dramatic composer, which he propounded to his hearers at Jena in 1790.

It is not this theory in its original form, however, that we have in the essays under consideration, which were not written out until the winter of 1791-2, *Über den Grund des Vergnügens an tragischen Gegenständen* in December,[75] and *Über die tragische Kunst* almost immediately afterwards, or after Schiller had devoted some study to the *Critique of Judgment* and Kant's moral treatises. The suggestion that the essays were already written, in part at least, during the year 1790, and merely worked over for publication at this time, has no weight, as Schiller had discontinued writing out his lectures before the summer semester of 1790. "My lectures do not give me much trouble now," he writes, February 1st, 1790; "I have given up working them out in full beforehand, and speak *extempore*. Thus I save several hours every day that I used to devote to writing them down, and the material is much better impressed upon my memory when I rely more upon it."[76]

Indeed, one is led to suspect, on reading these essays, that Schiller's mind was still better stocked with his own ideas than with the principles of the Kantian æsthetic. It is safe to say that he was at this time more impressed with the Kantian philosophy than he was enlightened by it. But that he had the firmest faith in its conclusions is put beyond doubt by the way in which he attempts to fit his own ideas to fundamental Kantian principles, both æsthetic and ethical. It was Kant's view of the nature of morality, in particular, that lent itself to Schiller's theory of the tragic, and it is this portion of Kant's philosophy that gained his almost complete adhesion at this time, as will be seen presently.

One of the first things that must strike the reader of these essays is the change of front on the subject of the function and purpose of art since he had last written on that subject, nearly a decade before. The function of art, he had said at that time, is twofold: the immediate one of relaxation and æsthetic enjoyment, and the ulterior and higher one of intellectual and moral improvement. The aim of nature, anyone must say who admits that nature has an aim at all, is the happiness of man, although — and here Schiller the Kantian speaks — although he ought to take no notice of this aim in his moral conduct. What the understanding yields only after labor and application, what the senses yield only at the risk of sacrifice or at the cost of privation, art procures for us in play and lavishes upon us as a pure gift. And as if speaking in direct criticism of his former essay, he says: "The praiseworthy object of pursuing everywhere moral good as the supreme aim, which has already brought forth in art so much mediocrity, has caused also in theory a similar prejudice. To assign to the fine arts a really elevated position, to win for them the favor of the state, the veneration of all men, they are pushed beyond their true domain, and a vocation is imposed upon them contrary to their nature. It is supposed that a great service is done them by substituting for a frivolous aim, that of charming, a moral aim; and their influence upon morality, which is so apparent, necessarily militates in favor of this pretension. It is found illogical that the art which contributes in so great a measure to the development of all that is most elevated in man should produce this effect only incidentally, and make its chief object an aim so vulgar as we imagine pleasure to be."

Schiller's view regarding the moral significance of art is perhaps nowhere put more clearly. Its value as an instrument of culture and of moral elevation is of the highest kind, but in order to be attained most fully, in order to have art at all, in fact, whose very essence is freedom, these must not be directly aimed at. The end of art is first and last to please, to excite æsthetic gratification, and all the other ends which this may bring in its train are defeated if this is lost sight of, just as the seeker after health or pleasure defeats his aim if he keeps his mind continually fixed upon the object of his search, instead of engaging in the living interests and activities of daily life, which are the indispensable means to the harmonious functioning of all one's powers in which health of body and mind consists.

The moral content of art, tragic art in particular, is explained by the fact that man is so thoroughly moral in his make-up, and that morality thus becomes the greatest source of æsthetic delight. Art, that is, cannot create the sources of pleasure, but must employ those that are already furnished and at hand. And it is in the exercise of the moral powers in the presence of moral situations furnished by art, Schiller holds, that these powers are strengthened and perfected. "The pleasure we find in the beautiful, pathetic and sublime strengthens our moral sentiments, as the pleasure we find in kindness, in love, etc., strengthens these inclinations." Besides, it seems to have been his belief that happiness as such was an important condition for the completest moral life. The coincidence of virtue, perfection and happiness was the optimistic creed of his earliest writings, and we found him working out rather elaborately the salutary influence upon man's physical nature of a happy condition of mind. The influence of virtue and happiness he thought of as reciprocal: just as contentment of mind must be the sure reward of the good man, so, on the other hand, moral excellence naturally flows from happiness and contentment of heart. This fundamental conviction may be traced in many of Schiller's first utterances; the unrest, the moral storm and stress evidenced in the dissonant poems *Freigeisterei* and *Resignation*, and other writings of the Dresden period, were due to the fact that it was for a time shaken, and it was this conviction that furnished the point of departure, in his final development, from the rigoristic and ascetic morality of the Kantian philosophy.

It is not within the intention of this chapter to follow Schiller through the details of æsthetic theory as developed in these essays, except in so far as these have a bearing upon his theory of morality, which, through the influence of Kant, is soon to take more definite form, and with which we shall now for some time be almost exclusively occupied. The æsthetic theory developed here is still vague and not at all representative of Schiller's later position, and can therefore not be advantageously treated except in its connection with the later and more purely æsthetic writings.

The definition and characterization of the tragic, however, as given here, are so firmly based upon, and illustrative of, Schiller's attitude on moral questions at this time, that some of his distinctions must be clearly brought out and fully grasped. The general source of æsthetic pleasure is *Zweckmässigkeit*, fitness or conformity to an end. Now this fitness is of two kinds: physical or natural fitness, and moral fitness. The pleasure produced by natural fitness must be distinguished again from merely sensuous pleasure, which is the result of a sensation awakened immediately by a physical cause, and which, as immediate and therefore necessitated, is excluded from the domain of art. Pleasure, to be æsthetic pleasure, must be "free," unrestrained, that is, by the law of natural necessity, and must bring into play the spiritual faculties of understanding, reason and imagination. Mere sense impression may be agreeable, but it cannot rise to the dignity of æsthetic pleasure so long as it remains merely sensuous; it is only in so far as sense impressions are given a formal or relational value, so as to be apprehended by representation, that they can afford æsthetic gratification.

In the valuation of natural and moral fitness as means to æsthetic ends the latter occupies the higher place. The reason Schiller gives for this is thoroughly Kantian. "Natural fitness could well be a problem, and a problem forever unsolvable. But moral fitness is already demonstrated. It alone is founded upon our reasonable nature and upon internal necessity. It is our nearest and most important interest, and at the same time the most easily recognized because it is not determined by any external element, but by an internal principle of our reason: it is the palladium of our liberty." While the true and the perfect are apprehended by the understanding, and the beautiful by the understanding and the imagination, the good is apprehended by reason, and the pathetic and sublime, *i. e.*, the good in conflict, by reason and the imagination. Indeed, a classification of the arts might be made upon the basis of the faculties which are employed in their apprehension, or upon the basis of the predominance, in any object of æsthetic contemplation, of natural or moral fitness. We should thus have the arts of the understanding, having for their principal object the true, the beautiful and the perfect, and the arts of reason or the heart, which have for their chief object the good, the sublime and the pathetic.

The Kantian influence is clearly seen in the emphasis placed upon the representation of fitness or purposiveness as the basis of æsthetic enjoyment, and in the entire exclusion from the sphere of the æsthetic of the purely sensuous element. The divisions of the faculties and the tendency to classification are, of course, thoroughly Kantian, and the definitions of the sublime and the pathetic are entirely in the spirit of the master. Indeed, the whole theory of tragedy, as here presented, rests upon, and the various kinds of tragedy may be tabulated on the basis of, the Kantian dualism between natural and moral forces, and the Kantian idea of fitness. For it is just in the sacrifice of a physical to a moral fitness, or in the sacrifice of one species of moral fitness to a higher one, in the subordination, in short, of the sensuous to ideal interests, that the tragic consists. Theron and Amanda are tied to the stake as martyrs; they are free to choose either life or death by the frightful ordeal of fire, but they choose the latter. The disregard of the natural interests awakens in us the feeling of unfitness, and ought to fill us with distress. But what are the discords in nature compared with the harmony in the world of moral freedom! The keen pleasure we feel in the contemplation of this scene is due to the fact that we see the triumph of moral fitness and of the moral law, an experience so sublime that we may even hail the calamity which elicits it. It is in such situations as this, in the struggle between the non-moral forces of nature, such as feelings, instincts, passions, physical necessity and destiny, with the moral law, that the latter is seen in its full power, and moral consciousness rises to the highest degree of clearness. "The more redoubtable the adversary, the more glorious the victory," and the more keen the pleasure we experience.

Schiller is disposed, we see here, to insist upon and carry through without qualification Kant's fundamental doctrine of the incompatibility of natural inclination and moral worth. And though he perhaps emphasizes more than did Kant the pleasure which accompanies virtuous action, yet this pleasure, however exalted it may be, is not the motive of the act, which must be different from natural inclination of any kind if the act is to have moral worth. So far he and Kant perfectly agree. Indeed, it seems almost as if Schiller were quoting Kant when he says that the moral merit of an act decreases just to the degree that it is determined by inclination or pleasure, or when he says in another place that it requires a clear understanding and a reason emancipated from the powers of nature to determine the relation of moral duties to the highest principle of morality.

That Schiller found the characterization of the tragic, as attempted in these essays, too narrow for his later thought, and that the entire exclusion, from the moral realm, of the desiderative side of man's nature proved sufficiently unsatisfactory to the poet to call forth some qualification, is, of course, familiar in a general way to any one at all acquainted with his later writings. But the elements of truth expressed here, however one-sided and incomplete they may have appeared to him at times in his later development, always made a strong appeal to the poet, both in his theoretical activity and in his work as artist. He was not so bad a moralist as to be willing to surrender the will to the solicitation of every passing desire of the agent, however unregulated or erratic that desire may be, nor was his sense of moral values so obscured as not to recognize the moral worth of an action, however fierce the conflict of the passions from which it emerged. It is in the conflicts of the moral life, in fact, that Schiller found the material for those dramatic situations which elicited his greatest powers, and on which the reader lingers with greatest pleasure. It is not the Piccolomini [77] who could "exercise in sport his duties, indulge all lovely instincts, act forever with undivided heart," that elicits our greatest sympathy and admiration. It is when "like enemies the roads start from each other, duties strive with duties," when he must choose his party in the war which is kindling between his friend and his emperor, when the beautiful, that is, rises to the sublime, that we feel the height of æsthetic enjoyment and the keenest interest. In the *Maid of Orleans*, too, and in *Mary Stuart*, the most powerful artistic effects are produced in those passages where, in the fierce conflict between the opposing forces of inclination and duty, or of the free spirit and blind fate, beauty rises into sublimity of action. Conflict, that is, and catastrophe form the very essence of a tragic situation, a conflict, of course, which, if it is to produce the highest æsthetic effect, must issue in the triumph of those interests which are regarded as of most significance or value. The subjective effect upon the observer will consist, as Schiller found, of a complex of painful and pleasurable emotions, painful through sympathy with the person or persons whose particular interests are sacrificed, and pleasurable through sympathy with the more universal and hence significant interests, moral or other, which are seen to triumph.

The tragic, we must conclude from passages in these essays, and from the thoroughly Kantian attitude in morality which he maintains here, Schiller regarded as the highest expression of dramatic art, at this period of his development. But the antagonisms and the oppositions which so deeply divide man against himself, we must imagine him to say at a later period of his artistic development, are not to be regarded as so permanent and absolute but that they may be softened down more and more as culture proceeds. The self and the not-self, the world of freedom and the world of necessity, are not so fundamentally different from each other but that, by a gradual process of transformation, the latter terms may be more and more embraced by the former. The art of the tragic, therefore, like the ethics of rigorism, will maintain its supremacy only at one stage in the development of humanity, a temporary period in a process which leads forward towards, though it may never completely attain to, that ideal condition in which there will be no "particularity of desire" to sacrifice, and hence no duty to triumph or conflict to harmonize. And as the cultivated man of to-day finds but little pleasure in the contemplation of the conflict of fierce passions as depicted in the poetry of primitive peoples, so the man of the future will find less and less pleasure in the contemplation of those moral conflicts which are the source of such deep satisfaction to man at the present stage of his moral development. The difference in tragic interest between the earlier works just mentioned and *William Tell*, which impresses the reader more by the placidity and lyric beauty of many of its parts than by its tragic situations, would suggest that Schiller became more enamored of that ideal of the conciliated self, which he proposed as the goal of æsthetic culture, as he approached the zenith of his artistic development, under the influence of Goethe.

The attempt of Schiller to free himself from the rigorous interpretation of morality as found in the essays just noticed, an interpretation we should not have expected from the reading of his early writings, and into which he was led, we must believe, in the first enthusiasm over the Critical Philosophy and by his great reverence for its founder, we must follow somewhat carefully in the next chapter. The main writings which will come under consideration are *Anmut und Würde* (1793), and, as supplementary to this, a group of poems of which the most notable are *Der Genius*, *Der Tanz*, and *Würde der Frauen*. References will also be made to *Über den moralischen Nutzen æsthetischer Sitten* and *Über die Gefahr æsthetischer Sitten*. The satirical epigrams *Gewissensscrupel* (*Xenien* 388) and *Decisum* (*Xenien* 389) may also be read in this connection. Then for Schiller's theory of education must be considered portions of *Briefe über die æsthetische Erziehung des Menschen* (1795), in connection with which may be read the poems *Die Künstler*, *Die Ideale*, and *Das Ideal und das Leben;* also *Tabula votiva*, 5-8, 47, and 57-60. As these are among the most widely known of the poet's works, and are included in almost every collection of his poems, it is not deemed necessary to offer any extended résumê of their contents. Our purpose, at any rate, will be best attained by leaving to one side the details, often pedantic and tiresome, of purely æsthetic theory, and by centering attention upon those passages which have an obvious bearing upon Schiller's view of morality in the final period of his development: for it is to ascertain this as definitely as possible that we must mainly devote ourselves from this time on.

CHAPTER VII

INDEPENDENT DEVELOPMENT

Attention has been called more than once to the fact that certain leading features of Schiller's later thought appear more or less clearly in the writings of the school period and in the other works which may be broadly designated as pre-Kantian: the stream of his thought, I have said, "was clarified and deepened, rather than directed into other channels, by contact with the Critical Philosophy." The one problem which seems to have been uppermost in his mind in the academic dissertations, particularly, but also in some of the minor writings both of his school period and afterwards, was to conciliate, as it were, the different factions or interests in human nature, and to offer some sort of mediating term by which the chasm which was supposed to exist between the natural and the spiritual, the physical and the moral, might be spanned. This middle term he had found in his metaphysical writings to be a substance which partook in a way of the character of both the physical and the spiritual, — *Mittelkraft* he called it, — at once penetrable and impenetrable, and thus at once susceptible of being acted upon by the material world and of acting upon spirit. He came early to inquire into the comparative importance of the mind and the body, and between the extreme idealists who regarded the body as only a prison-house of the spirit, checking its flight toward perfection, and the extreme materialists who treated knowledge and virtue as only a means to happiness, and who held that the whole perfection of man consists in "the amelioration and perfection of the body," Schiller was concerned to maintain an intermediate position; and, while holding spirit to be the higher term, he undertook to champion the rights of that part of our nature which, as he thought, had been underrated, and to show, by appealing to the actual development both of the individual and of the race as a whole, "the remarkable contribution of the body to the activity of the soul, and the great and real influence of the system of animal sensations upon the spiritual life." This great importance he found to consist not only in the function of the preservation of the organism which was entrusted to them, but in the fact that it was through the influence of these same animal feelings and impulses that man's spiritual nature is developed from its lowest and most primitive to its highest forms. Without these animal feelings, indeed, man's cognitive and, particularly, man's practical life would become an impossibility. Without feeling, no desire, and without desire no volition and no active life. Body, in short, is the indispensable companion of spirit in this present world: "Man has to be an animal before he can, like Newton, attempt the flight through the universe." Almost at the same time that we found Schiller trying to mediate between the natural and the spiritual by the metaphysical intermediate agent we had occasion to notice another attempt at this mediation by the forms of beauty. The problem here is the refinement and education of the primitive and merely natural instincts of the savage until they become instruments for the production of the noblest qualities of the human spirit. "Music softens the savage breast, beauty ennobles morals and taste, and art leads man to science and to virtue." In the essay on the moral influence of the stage, some four years later, the æsthetic condition is characterized as one of repose, a gentle harmony into which the tension due to the one-sided activity of our sensuous or our spiritual nature is resolved and the integrity of the true self is restored, and we found the author insisting in a rather one-sided way on the pedagogical value of art, recommending it in the highest terms as an instrument of intellectual and moral education. It is in the contemplation of art that there is induced that happy condition in which the spiritual is merged, as it were, with the natural, the former being humanized and softened, the latter refined and spiritualized in the process.

Having thus traced this rather persistent attempt of Schiller's to maintain an intermediate position between extreme sensualism and extreme rationalism in morality, we are prepared to anticipate the attitude which he will finally assume toward the extreme rigorism of the ethical system of Kant. That his attitude is that of independent criticism, and that it marks an advance upon the Kantian position, that this advance, finally, consists in a fuller recognition of the desiderative side of man's nature, all this must be the broad result of an unbiased reading of the writings of Schiller. The broad result: for when we come to determine the particular aspects of Schiller's moral doctrine, or attempt a definite formulation of his relation to Kant, the problem is by no means simple, and the reading of the different writings of the post-Kantian period yields no single or unambiguous result. Nor will a careful reading of the extensive literature which has been written on the Schiller-Kant problem help us materially. Writers of equal ability have arrived at the most diverse conclusions, from those who maintain that there is no essential difference between Kant and Schiller at any point of the latter's development, to those who find a radical and fundamental divergence between the two men's views from the outset, — a divergence which results in the complete repudiation, on the part of Schiller, of the moral point of view, in the sense of Kant, and in the substitution for this of a purely æsthetic ideal. The present writer's own attitude has already been indicated in the introductory chapter, and it must be his task in the present chapter to justify this position by a careful comparison of the different passages concerned.

The question is, to get the problem once more clearly before us, does Schiller conceive the progress of human development as passing from the natural through the æsthetic to the moral stage, that is, does he conceive the æsthetic condition as one in which man is freed from the bonds of physical necessity, and thus made capable of realizing his moral ideals, or is the progress rather from the natural through the moral stage to that final condition in which man is not merely natural or merely moral, but in which every part of his nature will have its due? If we find that the question cannot be answered one way or the other way without qualification, the clear formulation of it will at least aid us in the reading of the passages and in arriving at some sort of result.

The attitude of Schiller in *Anmut und Würde* is fairly clear and consistent, and will furnish a starting-point for the investigation of some of the later writings. One point of importance, however, must be clearly grasped at the outset, not only for the understanding of *Anmut und Würde* but for the correct interpretation of passages in some of the other writings with which we shall have to deal, and that is that two distinct kinds of valuation of human conduct must be recognized in Schiller, one from the standpoint of morality and the other from the purely æsthetic standpoint. The double demand which Schiller always makes of an act or a character is grounded upon the two fundamental traits, the artistic and the ethical, running through his entire nature, to which I have already adverted more than once. The full recognition of this dualism in point of view will help to clear up those passages in which Schiller seems prepared to accept without qualification the Kantian position that the only proper motive for a moral act is respect for the moral law, but in which he is no less intent on demanding recognition for those inclinations without which, as he somewhere says, the character can perform isolated moral acts, but can never attain to complete moral perfection.

Man, that is, has other than merely moral interests, and while for purposes of logical analysis or theoretical discussion we may separate man's moral interests from his æsthetic or what not, and pass judgment on an action or a character first from one point of view and then from another, such a separation is never actually made in practice, and man has as much right to demand that an act shall satisfy his æsthetic sense as that it shall measure up to the ideals of morality. And his æsthetic sense is never satisfied if the moral act is accomplished only after a severe conflict and at the sacrifice of a part of our entire nature. If such a struggle is inevitable, the artist, at least, has a right to demand that its ugly features and uncouth traces shall be hidden from his view. This twofold attitude which the spectator may assume toward human conduct is clearly illustrated by the whole tenor of Schiller's writings, and is explicitly recognized in more than one place. So in *Anmut und Würde*, after describing the expression reason requires of the human features as belonging to a moral being, he goes on to say: " But man as phenomenon is at the same time an object of sense, and when the *moral* feeling is satisfied, the æsthetic sense will not consent to a sacrifice of its own interests: the agreement with an idea must not lessen the beauty of the phenomenon. Thus, as much as reason demands an expression of morality, just as persistently does the eye demand beauty. Inasmuch, then, as both these requirements, though made by two distinct judgments, address themselves to the same object, both must be granted satisfaction by one and the same cause. The disposition of man which fits him best for fulfilling his mission as a moral being must also permit an expression that will be most advantageous to his beauty as a phenomenon. In other words, the aptitude of his moral activity ought to reveal itself by grace."[78]

Another precaution may not be out of place here, and may save us from much unnecessary confusion. I have just alluded to the fact that under conditions the moral struggle will be inevitable, and referred to the demands which the spectator may, even then, make of the agent in such a time of moral stress. Now a careful discrimination must always be made between those passages in which Schiller speaks of an ideal which is suited to our present state and which the conditions, as they exist here and now, permit us to realize, and an ideal, on the other hand, which man may approximate more and more, but which, owing to the limitations of human nature, is forever beyond the possibility of complete attainment. The distinction will be supported later by references to passages in point. It has been thought necessary to call attention to it explicitly at the outset, for it is only by a clear apprehension of it that we can hope to introduce some order and consistency into what may seem at first sight a hopeless confusion and a fundamental contradiction in Schiller's writings. Simply to ignore the difficulties, or to dismiss them by saying that Schiller espoused and rejected the Kantian doctrine in turn, at one time advocating a moral ideal and at another abandoning it for the æsthetic, is a quick and easy method, but indolent and essentially false. For while Schiller was not as systematic in his philosophical writings as he might have been, he was by no means a tyro in the discussion of the problems which interested him; and if he seems to contradict his own conclusions in places, it must be that he changes his point of view or speaks in different senses; and it becomes the duty of the student to determine by a careful study of the context what is the particular point of view adopted, and to point out definitely the sense in which the writer is speaking.

The complete blending of moral and æsthetic interests, to which attention has just been called, is nowhere seen more clearly than in *Anmut und Würde*, to the examination of which we must now address ourselves. Schiller was just fresh from his investigation into the nature of the beautiful, and had at length fixed upon the "objective principle upon which all taste is founded," and "which Kant had racked his brain about without success." Beauty, he announces to Körner, December, 1792, is nothing else than freedom-in-the-appearance (*Freiheit in der Erscheinung*). And in succeeding letters he attempts to apply his new discovery to an exposition of the relation between the objects of beauty in nature and art, and the æsthetic observer. In order to be beautiful the object must not appear to suffer any determination from without, but must convey, by its form, a suggestion of freedom. A law indeed there is, but it is the law of the object's own nature, and each beautiful object thus represents, as it were, a kingdom of freedom. A vase is beautiful when it seems to suffer no restraint, but in its gracefulness gives the appearance of a free play of its own nature. A birch is beautiful when it is slender and graceful, an oak when it is rugged and bent: the sight of a slender oak or a distorted birch could not but offend the eye, because such shapes would be contrary to the nature of the objects: they would seem to be determined from without.

This theory he attempts to apply also to his favorite subject of morality. The concept of beauty is too general, however, when applied to the human being, with his dual nature. We must here distinguish between fixed beauty which man has in common with other natural objects, and mobile beauty, *i. e.*, beauty of voluntary movements "which express some sentiment of the *moral order*." Merely natural movements like the undulations of the ringlets of hair on a beautiful head cannot pretend to it, nor even voluntary or instinctive movements, so long as they are expressions of our merely sensuous nature. It is this beauty of movement, this graciousness of behavior, the outward expression of an inner harmony, that Schiller calls *Anmut*. It is a personal quality, may be acquired or forfeited, and if sympathetic, *i. e.*, not directly aimed at, may become the truest test of character and moral worth. "Architectonic beauty does honor to the author of nature; grace does honor to him who possesses it. The former is a gift, the latter a personal merit."

So far Schiller has spoken of grace as a quality of movement, and has contrasted it with fixed or architectonic beauty, which is a product of necessity. But he goes on to modify his position somewhat, and grants that features fixed and in repose may also possess grace. This he explains, however, as due to the frequent repetition of graceful movements, as the durable traces or the crystallized form of habitual beauty of conduct; and since it thus represents the *aptitude* of the soul for beautiful feeling, even esteems it, of all the species of grace, the most precious.[79] Schiller, we see here, is approaching a favorite subject of his earliest metaphysical speculations, and what he says here about the beautifying or distorting effect of the feelings and passions upon the physical features affords an interesting parallel to the remarks he made on the same subjects nearly a decade before.

We are now fairly in possession of the critical apparatus with which Schiller met the Kantian morality; and when he goes further and states explicitly that in order to have grace or beauty of conduct no sort of restraint must be exerted either by the will or by passion, by spirit or by nature, one feels that the decisive word has been spoken, and that it needs only the moral to complete the tale. The action which is prompted solely by respect for the moral law is good as far as it goes; and there are times when such action is demanded. But it does not fulfil the conditions which Kant himself demanded of moral activity, namely, that it shall be self-determined. One kind of slavery is just as humiliating as another, and perfect freedom is found only when the act proceeds from the character of man in its entirety: from a character in which reason and sense, inclination and law, are in perfect harmony. The ideal moral organization is that in which nature is so thoroughly disciplined that it executes with ease and precision those actions which, if it were not so disciplined, reason would, in its capacity as intelligence, be obliged to demand. *Inclination to duty,* — that is the heart of Schiller's ethics, and the gist of his criticism of Kantian rigorism.

Schiller is never tired of trying to enforce his favorite thought, and he repeats it in a variety of ways and enforces it by a number of telling illustrations. We can conceive of a threefold relation, he says, in which the sensuous part of man's nature can stand to his reason. Man may either repress the demands of sense in order to live conformably to his reason, or he may subordinate the reasonable portion of his being to the sensuous, and allow himself to be swept away, like other merely natural objects, by the force of physical necessity; or, finally, the inclinations may place themselves in harmony with law, and man is one with himself.[80] The beauty of conduct of which we are in search is not found in the first case, for where the sensuous nature offers an obstinate and vigorous resistance it must be met by a similar resistance on the part of spirit; but under this stern discipline sensuousness will appear repressed, and the inner conflict will reveal itself outwardly by constraint. A condition of pure morality, then, cannot be favorable to beauty of action, which nature cannot produce except in so far as it is perfectly free; and we can never have grace of action so long as there are visible the traces of the conflict between moral freedom and the material conditions. Still less do we find beauty of action in the second case. Whereas under the rule of reason the freedom of form was only restrained, here it is completely crushed by the brutal force of matter. Here the inner autonomy has vanished, and every external trace of this autonomy is entirely effaced. The grim realism with which Schiller describes the wretched witnesses of this physical and moral degradation, — the dull, protruding eye, the relaxed lips and stupid mouth, the gasping voice and irregular breath, — reveals at once the medical student and the sensitive observer to whom the human form was the emblem and expression of all that was most precious in life. "Man in this condition not only revolts the *moral* sense . . . but the *æsthetic* sense also, which is not content with mere matter, but seeks true pleasure in form, will turn away from such a spectacle with disgust."

"Of these two relations between the moral nature of man and his physical nature, the first makes one think of a monarchy where the strict surveillance of the ruler restrains every spontaneous movement; the second resembles an ochlocracy in which the citizen, in refusing obedience to his legitimate sovereign, finds he has liberty quite as little as the human features have beauty when the moral autonomy is suppressed. . . . Now just as *liberty* is found between the extremes of legal oppression and anarchy, so also we shall find *beauty* between dignity, which bears witness to the domination exercised by mind, and voluptuousness, which reveals the domination of instinct." [81]

This comparison between the relation of the parts of man's nature and the relation of the governing and the governed in the state calls to mind the almost identical comparison drawn by Plato. It may be interesting to call attention in this connection to the very close resemblance between Schiller's *Anmut* and Plato's *Justice,* which is precisely that equable arrangement or right relation of its single parts or powers in which the completed perfection of the soul consists. This anticipation by the reason of the wants of nature, and by nature of the laws of reason may be further illustrated by the relation Leibniz maintains to exist between the governing monad and the governed, soul and body, as we call them, in organic nature. When we speak of a ruling or a governing monad, Leibniz warns us, the expression is merely figurative, for by virtue of the autonomy of each monad, of whatever degree of development, this dominating influence of the ruling monad is purely ideal. We cannot speak of rule or domination in the literal sense if the obedience of the governed monads is, as indeed it is, entirely spontaneous. "They do not subordinate themselves to the ruling monad because this forces them to do so, but because their own nature compels them to do it." The illustration by reference to Leibniz may not be inapt, since we know that the Leibnizian metaphysics exerted a strong influence over Schiller especially during the earlier periods of his philosophical activity, and we find distinct traces of the Leibnizian view of nature as late as the time of the *Philosophical Letters,* in which Raphael points out to Julius that the difference between the human and the divine artist is that, while the former governs despotically over his material, the latter respects the individuality and worth of every part of his handiwork, and that "the respect with which he honors every germ of energy even in the lowliest creature, glorifies him just as much as the harmony of the immeasurable whole." And when Raphael adds that life and freedom characterize every part of the divine creation, we feel that he could hardly have expressed more clearly the central motive of Schiller's ethical philosophy. It is not until reason is so completely humanized that it will render due respect to nature, and nature is so completely rationalized that it will execute spontaneously the behests of reason, not till subjection, in short, gives place to perfect freedom, and man is at peace with himself, that the ideal of humanity has been fully realized. The conduct flowing from such a harmonious activity of all man's powers Schiller calls beautiful conduct (*die schöne Sittlichkeit*), and the soul thus at one with itself the beautiful soul (*die schöne Seele*).

The criticism of the Kantian morality with which Schiller follows up the delineation of his own ideal of "beautiful morality" is characteristic, and shows in every line the great reverence which he has for the master, a reverence which doubtless kept him, at this time, from going the full extent of his convictions in his opposition to the Kantian rigorism. "In the moral philosophy of Kant," he says, "the idea of duty is expounded with a harshness which is enough to frighten away the Graces, and could easily tempt a feeble mind to seek for moral perfection in the somber paths of an ascetic and monkish life. However much the great philosopher may have endeavored to guard against this false interpretation, which must be repugnant more than all else to so cheerful and independent a mind, he has nevertheless given occasion for it, as it seems to me, by placing in such strict and harsh opposition the two principles which act upon the human will." The meaning of Kant, Schiller thinks, is perfectly justifiable, and the conclusions which Kant reached were reached on "purely objective grounds:" it was only when he came to the *exposition* of the truths he had gained that he appears to have been "guided by more subjective maxims," which, Schiller believes, can be easily explained by the circumstances of the time. The shallow morality of the period, manifesting itself under the forms of coarse materialism, perfectionism and sensualism, needed some heroic remedy, and Kant applied it. It was not *ignorance* that he had to deal with, but *perversion.* "The cure required violent measures, not persuasion or flattery; and the more violent the contrast between the truth and the dominant maxims, the more he could hope to provoke reflection. He was the Draco of his time because his time seemed to him as yet unworthy and unprepared for a Solon. From the sanctuary of pure reason he drew forth the strange and yet so familiar moral law, and troubled himself little to know whether there were eyes too enfeebled to bear the brightness."[82]

But what have the children of the house done, he adds, that Kant should make provision only for the valets? It is true, as Kant holds, that inclination is often an uncertain guide, and may prompt to the evil as well as to the good. But must we on that account reject it altogether? "Because impure inclinations usurp the name of virtue, is that a reason why the disinterested feelings in the noblest heart should also be placed under suspicion? Because the moral weakling would make the law lax enough to suit all his whims and caprices, there is no reason to give it a rigidity which would turn the most spontaneous expression of moral freedom into slavery. Under this imperative of the law the pure will is under no less restraint than the depraved: man is accused and humbled, and the law which ought to be the most sublime witness of our grandeur becomes the most crushing argument for our frailty. The law which man has imposed upon himself comes, by this imperative form, to have the aspect of a positive law imposed from without, an appearance which is not entirely unjustified by the alleged radical tendency in human nature to act in opposition to it."

The reference here is to Kant's doctrine of radical evil, developed in a paper with that caption published in the *Berliner Monatsschrift*, April, 1792, and afterwards embodied in his *Religion innerhalb der Grenzen der blossen Vernunft*, published at Easter, 1793. Schiller, it appears, read advance sheets of it as early as February 28th, 1793. The work, he writes to Körner on that date, "has carried me away, and I can scarcely await the remaining sheets. One of the first principles laid down, however, is revolting to my feelings, and will probably be so to yours. He maintains an inborn propensity of the human heart to evil, which he calls radical evil, and which is by no means to be confounded with the solicitations of sense. He places it above sense in the *personality* of man, the seat of freedom. But you will read it for yourself. It is impossible to refute his arguments, however much one might desire to do so."[83]

The question whether reason as such can supply a motive to action, — a question which has come in for so large a share of attention in modern ethical literature, and a consideration of which would seem to be of first importance in any discussion of the Kantian morality, — was not overlooked by Schiller, though he does not seem to have been sufficiently impressed with its importance to discuss it at length. The will, he remarks, stands in a more immediate relation to feeling than it does to cognition, and it would be in a bad plight if it had to appeal to pure reason in every case for guidance. At any rate, he is almost ready to suspect the man who can trust his instinct so little that he must bring it before the bar of the moral law on every occasion. The man whom we esteem most highly is the man who can surrender himself to his impulse, and who need not be in constant fear of being led astray by it. "That he can do this is evidence that the two principles of his nature have already attained that condition of harmony which is the seal of completed humanity, and constitutes the *beautiful soul.*"

It would seem from the doubt which Schiller casts upon the efficiency of reason when compared with feeling to supply a motive for effective action, especially in times of moral emergency, that he proposed his ideal of disposition and character in the interests of morality as well as in the interests of æsthetics. Just as that state is never secure which is based upon force rather than upon liberal principles, so morality is not secure so long as the triumph of one faction of man's nature depends upon the suppression of another. "It is only," he says in a rather striking passage, "when man's moral attitude results from the united action of the two principles and thus becomes the expression of *his entire humanity*, — *when it becomes his second nature*, — that it is secure; for as long as the spirit employs violence, so long must instinct use force to resist it. The enemy who is only overpowered and *cast down* can rise again, but the enemy who is *reconciled* is truly vanquished." [84]

As much, however, as Schiller is disposed to

claim for the moral instinct and for beautiful conduct on behalf of objective morality and in the name of taste, he is never willing to allow that any moral worth attaches to them. On this point he and Kant are in complete agreement. The phenomenal value of an act, its value, that is, from the standpoint of the æsthetic observer (and from the standpoint, perhaps, of objective morality), may therefore be in an inverse ratio to its moral value in the sense of Kant. It is important to notice this, for to misunderstand Schiller here would be not only to do injustice to his position, but to misunderstand his relation to the attitude of Kant. And if a few passages occur which appear to lend countenance to a contrary position, these must be neglected, as being opposed to the plain letter of many passages throughout the writings with which we are dealing.[85] Schiller maintains, as was said at the outset, the Kantian distinction between legal and moral, the only difference being that, for reasons already adverted to, Schiller is inclined to rate legal conduct much more highly than Kant, from his more restricted point of view, was enabled to do.

In thus waiving any claim to the value or merit (*Verdienst*) of an act when it appears as the result of natural inclination or a good disposition, and is judged independently of its material consequences, Schiller is no doubt justified by common usage. Just as we do not say that a man has merited or earned external possessions or personal talents which have come to him through inheritance or as a gift of nature, without any expenditure of energy on his part, so we do not attribute merit, or, to use a term with perhaps a still stricter signification, and corresponding more nearly with the German *Verdienst*, we do not attribute desert to an action for the performance of which is required no expenditure of energy or sacrifice on the part of the agent. The double judgment which we pass on conduct, first from the point of view of the sacrifice involved or the energy expended in its production, second from the point of view of its material consequences (a judgment which, as has been shown, may be still further complicated by æsthetic considerations), finds an interesting parallel in economics where an object is valuated on the basis (1) of the cost of production, or the effort or sacrifice made for it, and (2) of its utility. It is just on account of this constant association between sacrifice and meritorious action that by a common confusion of thought what is a necessary means or a concomitant of the means often comes to be regarded in the light of an end worthy of pursuit for its own sake, and that any action, if only it involves sacrifice or effort, is assumed to have moral value. Thus fasting, as Simmel points out,[86] though originally adopted merely as a means to spiritual ends, came as early as the time of Tertullian to possess an independent religious value, and self-denial and ascetic practices of all kinds, because recurring as the constant element in virtuous actions of the most various kinds, have often been regarded as highly meritorious. And when one reads Schiller's *Würde der Frauen,* in which he contrasts the unconscious grace, the beautiful harmony, of the character of woman with the unruly and tempestuous temper of the sterner sex, one is reminded that the term *virtuous,* etymologically considered, is perhaps more significant than might at first thought be supposed. The conduct, at any rate, which is deemed virtuous in the sense of meritorious by the moral judgment of to-day, though not distinctly associated with man, is nevertheless that conduct which emerges, not from the harmonious disposition, but from that conflict of opposing forces in which the manly or heroic traits of humanity find their completest manifestation.

After making the Kantian distinction between legal and strictly moral acts, and placing himself in complete agreement, as he says, with the rigorists in morality by denying feeling any voice "in the sphere of pure reason," it seems almost like taking back his own statement when he goes on to declare that the very feeling which "can prove nothing regarding the morality of the act" is indispensable to the moral perfection of man. "For man," he adds, "is not intended to accomplish isolated moral acts, but to be a moral being. It is not *virtues* that are prescribed to him, but *virtue*, and virtue is nothing else than inclination to duty."

The suggestion that a constitution of character which keeps man from performing moral acts is yet indispensable for his complete morality, paradoxical as it may seem, is perhaps also justified by common usage. Just as we do not attribute desert to the performance of physical feats by an athlete whose physical powers and training enable him to accomplish them without strain or a painful expenditure of energy, while yet willing to assign a high degree of merit, perhaps, to the athlete for having undertaken the long series of tedious exercises which we assume to have been necessary for arriving at his present condition of physical excellence, so likewise we do not commonly attribute a high moral quality to those acts, during the time of their performance, which we feel have been "natural," and have involved little or no individual cost, while at the time we value highly, even aside from his material worth to society or his æsthetic significance, the person himself, who embodies, as it were, and represents the long series of more or less heroic and disciplinary acts which have made possible that ease and grace of action which flows from a highly cultivated moral disposition. It is this tendency to value "virtues," *i. e.*, isolated moral acts, rather than "virtue" and personality, that justifies in a way the complaint often heard by the "beautiful" child or the good citizen, that he is not appreciated as much as his meaner brother or neighbor, whose virtues, like the single stars, shine only the more brightly for their isolation. It was the son, in the parable, who had wasted his substance in riotous living that received the ring and the robe and shoes and ate of the fatted calf, while the son who had served many years and had not at any time transgressed had to content himself with those slight tokens of affection which, though perhaps more than making up for their slightness by the frequency of their occurrence, were less appreciated, no doubt, on account of their very commonness. And when we are assured by the sacred text that there shall be more joy in heaven over one sinner that repents than over ninety and nine just persons who need no repentance, we understand that the rejoicing is over the single act of repentance, and the future conduct for which it is the guarantee, rather than over the personality of the sinner, who certainly cannot on any standard of valuation be esteemed more highly than ninety and nine just persons who need no repentance. We surely do not consider that in the long run we raise ourselves in the esteem of others by plunging into dissipation, though the disapproval from which we suffer is to a certain extent removed, and our loss of moral esteem to a degree compensated for, by the rejoicing on the occasion of our return to the moral fold.

However much verbal agreement there may be between Schiller and Kant on the matter of morality and legality, it is after all the difference between the two men that strikes the reader as important, and this difference, broadly stated, consists in the circumstance, as I conceive the matter, that Kant was interested almost exclusively in "morality," while Schiller's interest lay primarily in "legality." Kant had regard for the subjective motive, the letter and the form; Schiller, for the material effect, the spirit and the life. While Kant had unbounded confidence in the power of reason, and was jealous of its prerogatives, regarding feeling as an incompetent and dangerous guide to the will, Schiller was rather inclined to doubt the capacity of reason, considered in independence of the emotional nature, to furnish a sufficient motive for conduct, and had unlimited confidence, on the other hand, in the possibility of the education of feeling to the point where the will might surrender itself completely to its guidance, and have no occasion to fear for the consequences. It was the "children of the house" whom Kant had neglected for the valets, those exquisite souls that have been purged of fierce passions and conflicting interests, whose quick and sensitive instincts shrink from the coarse and unbeautiful in conduct, and furnish guidance through those complex moral situations whose finer points reason is unable to discern, and law too cumbrous to decide; for whom, in short, duty has become a grateful task:

"Glad hearts! without reproach or blot;
Who do thy work, and know it not:"

it was these who, after all, came in for the largest share of Schiller's interest.

It is the beautiful soul that the poet celebrates in a number of poems whose dash and finish bear witness to the enthusiasm with which he contemplated this ideal of his poetic nature. In the choice between reason and uncorrupted feeling it was always the latter that received Schiller's favor and support. "Know'st thou," he warns the youth who is about to distrust his heart and seek guidance of reason,

"Know'st thou what bars thy way? how dear the bargain thou dost make
When but to buy uncertain good, sure good thou dost forsake?

Feel'st thou sufficient strength to brave the deadliest human fray —
When Heart from Reason — Sense from Thought, shall rend themselves away?

. . . .

Fly, if thou canst not trust thy heart to guide thee on the way —
Oh! fly the charmed margin, ere the abyss engulf its prey.
Round many a step that seeks the light the shades of midnight close;
But in the glimmering twilight, see — how safely childhood goes!"[87]

The complete blending of freedom and law is symbolized in the well-known poem *Der Tanz*, whose noble ease and smoothly flowing rhythm is itself the best illustration of the ideal it glorifies. The buoyant movement of the dance, "like the skiff that softly rocks when silver waves are fair," represents primarily the entire domain of the fine arts, in which submission to rule and glad freedom of expression are united as in the playful movements of the dance forms. And as in art we obey the law of nature with gladness, so also should it be in conduct, which, from one point of view, may be considered as one of the fine arts, and not the least noble. Perhaps the most significant of these poems, from a philosophical standpoint, though less perfect in workmanship than the piece just mentioned, is *Der Genius*, at first perhaps more appropriately called *Natur und Schule*. Can knowledge only and the wooden systems, the question runs, lead to true peace? Must I mistrust impulse, the law which nature herself has written in my bosom, unless it squares with the rule,

> "Till the school's signet stamp the eternal scroll,
> Till in one mold some dogma hath confined
> The ebb and flow, the light waves, of the mind?
> Say thou, familiar to these depths of gloom,
> . . . .
> Say — if life's comfort with yon mummies dwells!
> Say — and I grope — with saddened steps indeed —
> But on, through darkness, if to Truth it lead!"

Friend, the answer runs, you remember the golden time

> "When heavenlier shapes with man walked side by side,
> And the chaste feeling was itself a guide
> . . . .
> Then sense unerring — because unreproved —
> True as the finger on the dial moved,
> Half guide, half playmate, of earth's age of youth,
> The sportive instinct of eternal truth."

But this golden time is gone, and desecrated feeling is no more the voice of the gods. Nature now yields her truth only to the inquirer who seeks it with a pure heart. But, the genius adds, if thou hast not lost thy guardian angel from thy side, if thy heart's guileless childhood can yet rejoice in sweet instinct with its warning voice, then go hence in thy innocence:

> "Science can teach thee naught — she learns from thee!
> . . . .
> From thine own self thy rule of action draw;
> That which thou dost — what charms thee — is thy law."

These thoughts are repeated in endless variety, and may be found in many places, both in the shorter poems and in the dramas. One or two of the *Votive Tablets* may be reproduced in conclusion.

For the following I have not found an adequate translation, and therefore reproduce it in the original:

> "Über das Herz zu siegen ist gross, ich verehre den Tapfern;
> Aber wer durch sein Herz sieget, er gilt mir doch mehr."

From the last poem Schiller wrote, *Die Huldigung der Künste:*

> "Doch Schön'res find' ich nichts, wie lang ich wähle,
> Als in der schönen Form — die schöne Seele."

But this ideal of completed humanity, we learn from several very explicit statements, is only a task, which is forever beyond the reach of perfect fulfilment. "It has indeed been prescribed to man," he says at the beginning of the second part of *Anmut und Würde,* — "to bring about a complete union of his two natures, and to form a harmonious whole, so as to be able to act with his entire humanity. But this beauty of character, the last fruit of his humanity, is but an idea, to conform to which he can strive with constant vigilance, but to which he can with all his efforts never completely attain."

The reason for this lies in the natural limitations of humanity incident to the dependence of its existence upon natural conditions. Nature, unwilling to entrust so momentous a matter as the preservation of the individual and the race to man's doubtful intelligence, has provided him with instinct which impels him, by an almost inevitable necessity, to avert those situations which threaten his existence, and to seek those which make for his preservation and well-being. And though it is the prerogative and the glory of man to be able to rise superior to his momentary desires, yet in its own sphere feeling must always continue to hold powerful sway, and to demand the recognition and respect even of reason. The possibility, therefore, of a conflict between the law of spirit and the law of nature is never entirely excluded. When this conflict, however, occurs, when nature takes the will by surprise, as it were, and tries to force it to yield allegiance to her, the moral character must manifest itself by its resistance, and "in order to keep from being restrained by instinct, must restrain the instinct itself." In these cases beauty of action, which is impossible when inclination and law are thus at war, rises into grandeur or sublimity, and "dignity" is its expression in appearance. It is in these times of stress that the difference between merely temperamental conduct and beautiful conduct clearly reveals itself. In the merely temperamental character, in whom inclination is on the side of duty simply because duty is accidentally on the side of inclination, the will will yield to the force brought to bear upon it by sense, and if any sacrifice is to be made it will itself be obliged to make it. The beautiful soul, on the other hand, which has merely entrusted sense, as it were, with the guidance of conduct, will take back this trust the moment nature seems inclined to abuse it; sense, as the lower term, must subordinate itself to reason, and beautiful action will rise to the sublime.[88] Schiller speaks in places as if the union of *Anmut* and *Würde* in the same person were the mark of human perfection, and as if he proposed this as the ideal of completed humanity. So in *Anmut und Würde:* "When grace and dignity . . . are united in the same person the expression of humanity would be completed in him: such a person would stand justified in the intelligible world and acquitted in the natural."[89] So also in *Über das Erhabene*[90] he speaks as if the development of the ability to act sublimely must be a part of æsthetic education, as well as the development of the ability to act in accordance with the demands of taste. But the meaning we must attach to these passages, in the light of Schiller's other and apparently contradictory utterances, is that along with the education of the natural instincts there must go such an education of the moral feelings that if nature should at any time fail us, as it almost inevitably will in human experience, we may still have recourse to the imperative of the moral law. It cannot be the task of æsthetic education "to bring about a complete union of man's dual nature" so that he can act with his entire humanity, and, at the same time, to develop "grace" and "dignity" side by side; and if Schiller speaks of the complete fusion of man's natural and moral powers and their due coördination, it may be, as the mark of human perfection, he must speak of human perfection in different senses. And this indeed he does, as has been pointed out. The difference is that between an absolute ideal, a poet's dream, forever beyond the reach of realization in consequence of the conditions of existence and the limitations of our humanity, and an ideal, on the other hand, which lies within man's possibilities, and the attainment of which constitutes his highest trust. The difference between the ideal and the actual demand made upon humanity is clearly brought out by placing side by side the passage in the *Æsthetic Letters* in which the author says that "man must learn to desire more nobly in order that he may have no need to act sublimely," and the passage in *Votive Tablets* to the effect that if man cannot desire in accordance with the demands of beauty he will nevertheless have it within his power to act in accordance with reason, and so do in his capacity as spirit what lies beyond the power of his humanity.

The poetic expression of this human ideal, as we may call it, is found in the poem *Die Führer des Lebens*, which on account of its brevity may be reproduced in full:

> "Two genii are there, from thy birth through weary life to guide thee;
> Ah, happy when, united both, they stand to aid, beside thee!
> With gleesome play, to cheer the path, the one comes blithe with beauty —
> And lighter, leaning on his arm, the destiny and duty.
> With jest and sweet discourse, he goes unto the rock sublime,
> Where halts above the eternal sea, the shuddering child of Time.
> The other here, resolv'd and mute, and solemn claspeth thee,
> And bears thee in his giant arms across the fearful sea.
> Never admit the one alone! — Give not the former guide
> Thy honor — nor unto the last thy happiness confide!"

It remains to speak briefly of Schiller's rather famous theory of æsthetic education by means of which, according to Schiller's sanguine view, man's complete culture was to be achieved. The education of man through the instrumentality of art was a favorite subject of reflection, as has been seen, from his earliest writings to the last. It was touched upon in the school essays, discussed rather elaborately in the essays on the influence of the stage, and given poetic expression in *Die Künstler*, which has been justly ranked among Schiller's noblest poems. The subject is taken up again in a more extended way in the *Letters on Æsthetic Education*, published in 1795. It would be impossible in the short space at our disposal to give an adequate idea of the wealth of this, perhaps the most original and interesting of all Schiller's prose writings, and we shall have to content ourselves with a brief examination of the subject Schiller proposes to discuss, leaving aside the many pregnant observations on political and purely æsthetic subjects as being beyond our immediate interest. The truth is that while the *Letters* cover over a hundred pages, Schiller never fairly faces his problem, and he discusses it even more scantily than it deserves.

The purely sensuous condition, we are told, is one of restraint, and it becomes the first care of the moral pedagogue to break the power of sense, so that man may be enabled to fulfil his vocation as a moral being. The instrument or agency by which this is accomplished is art. "It is one of the most important objects of culture to subject man in his purely physical existence to the influence of form . . . to make him æsthetic, because it is only from the æsthetic condition, not from the physical, that man can pass into a state of morality."[91] Not that the æsthetic condition is of any positive and direct significance either for knowledge or for the will: it is perfectly indifferent and fruitless; it discovers not a single idea and helps to fulfil not a single duty. All it does is to give man back to himself, as it were, to restore his freedom so that he can make of himself what he will. In the æsthetic condition, as Schiller likes to express it, man is zero, but he is thus prepared to become all things; and small as the gift may seem that art bestows on man, it is really infinite. In this condition man in void of interest (*interesselos*), in the language of Kant; both the sensuous and the moral needs are cancelled, for the time being, and the transition from the physical to the moral state thus becomes a possibility. Kant,[92] too, regarded the new birth, the transition, that is, from nature to morality, as an inexplicable act of the intelligible character. But the aid which Kant sought in religion Schiller sought to supplement by invoking the agency of art; it will be remembered that in the essays on the moral influence of the stage Schiller placed art, religion and law side by side, and found in art, even then, an instrument superior to the other two in accomplishing the work of regenerating man.

It may be doubted, if we emphasize too much the passages in which Schiller dwells upon the merely negative character of the æsthetic condition, whether he could claim for art a place equal or even superior to religion as an instrument of moral education. The claims of religion and the claims Schiller makes for art are indeed very similar. Religion,[93] too, claims to reduce the merely "natural" inclinations of man to a minimum, so that his "spiritual" nature may have an opportunity, as it were, to assert itself. But it claims more than this merely negative merit: whatever may be thought of the religious sanctions as permanent and indispensable adjuncts to the machinery of moral education, there is no question that they have furnished important positive motives for morality in the past, and will doubtless continue to do so among certain large classes of religious persons for some time to come. At any rate, whether the dynamic is to come from religion or what not, it is certain that man's morality will not be secured by reducing his desiderative activity to a minimum so that the moral law may have an opportunity to exert its power. This is, to say the least, an unfortunate way of putting the matter. Schiller is never at his best in the more theoretical formulation of his principles, and we may feel free, we take it, since Schiller has himself put the matter in different ways, not to insist unduly upon the passages in the *Æsthetic Letters* just adverted to. It is not the intention of the poet, we must say in the light of all his previous philosophical endeavors, to subtract from human nature, but rather to transform and utilize what is furnished and at hand. And this is what æsthetic education, according to the whole tenor of Schiller's philosophy, tends to do. The function of art as an instrument of education at first appears as in no wise different from that of religion: its appeal, as Schiller put the matter in the essays on the moral influence of the stage, is largely to man's hopes and fears: and it accomplishes its purpose the more perfectly because it employs not dogmas whose truth is questionable, or sanctions which are too far removed in the future to have any large degree of moral influence, but because it brings before men's very eyes, in the living images of sense, the charm of virtue and the hideousness of vice, and presents in concrete form the natural rewards and punishments which these entail. This crass and rather uncharacteristic way of stating the case is nowhere found, so far as I have seen, in Schiller's later writings, where he tends rather to speak of the refining influence of æsthetic objects upon man's nature, so that the unbeautiful, or, what always means the same thing for Schiller, the immoral, will lose its attraction for him, and the beautiful or moral will have more powerful sway. *Bildung*, that is, is simply *Um-*

bildung, education is transformation, or a reorganization, we might say, of man's motives. This is certainly the least that Schiller would say. So far from limiting man's desiderative and rational life and reducing him to a condition of pure passivity, it is rather the function of art to develop every part of man's nature to its utmost extent, so that he may live not less but more: his sensuous nature, as the poet rather strikingly puts it in one place, that he may apprehend (*ergreifen*) more, and his rational that he may comprehend (*begreifen*) more.

Precisely how this refinement and development of man's nature is accomplished by art Schiller thought it unnecessary, or, what seems more likely from his own confession about the difficulty of writing those portions of the *Letters* in which he approaches the problem, found it difficult to state. He has thrown out suggestions in other parts of his writings which may aid us in forming some sort of idea how the matter presented itself to his mind, and which may accordingly be brought together in this place. We have found him emphasizing (1) the importance of the relaxation of man's powers, especially after having been one-sidedly employed; and this relaxation, he conceived, was afforded in its purest form in æsthetic contemplation, where all the parts of man's nature receive their due, as in play. (2) Art, especially in tragic situations, affords an opportunity for the exercise of man's moral powers, particularly, which may thus be trained and strengthened. (3) It was Schiller's view that a condition of happiness or contentment is in general conducive to that physical and spiritual well-being which is an indispensable requisite for the fullest moral life, and this condition of physical well-being and spiritual exaltation, we may imagine him to say, it is at least one of the functions of art to induce. To these general propositions, I suppose, no serious objection will be made, if only their importance is not exaggerated. The influence upon conduct of æsthetic habituation, as we may call it, or the development of taste through the contemplation of objects of æsthetic value, will also, perhaps, not be questioned. It is no doubt due to the more refined æsthetic sensibilities of the Greeks that they never descended to those depths of moral degradation into which the coarser nature of the Romans permitted the latter to fall.

Nor is it necessary that the moral influence of taste be a merely negative or restraining one: it is possible to conceive that the æsthetic nature may be so thoroughly developed and completely refined that "beautiful action," in the sense of Schiller, those more or less typical moral situations which satisfy the moral demand, may exercise a strong and positive influence over the agent. Just as the moral imperative comes to exercise greater and greater influence over us as moral education proceeds, impelling us not merely to recognize an act as moral, but also to do it, so the æsthetic imperative, as we may call it, may develop sufficient dynamic, as æsthetic education proceeds, to impel us not only to acknowledge conduct as beautiful, but also to realize it, in some degree, by our own efforts. The two imperatives doubtless combine in determining the actual conduct of the average moral person at any stage of his cultural development. The moral influence of the products of the religious imagination, we may say, in so far as they do not appeal merely to the instinct of fear, is due almost entirely to the æsthetic elements they contain. Indeed, it is hard for one to see how it could be otherwise, if one accepts the view that a large part of the images and ideals of the religious imagination are but the crystallization and ideal construction of those portions of human experience which have stirred most profoundly the emotional nature.

CHAPTER VIII

THE RELATION OF SCHILLER TO POST-KANTIAN IDEALISM

The position of Schiller in the history of modern ethics and æsthetics has often been explained by philosophical writers, and his solid merits in these fields may be said to be to-day generally recognized. In the philosophy of art, his theory of the æsthetic state as one in which the various powers of man's nature come into spontaneous and balanced play, his definition of beauty as freedom-in-the-appearance, his ethical concept of the beautiful soul (*die schöne Seele*) in which the harsh opposition between inclination and duty is resolved, and man is at peace with himself, his theory of the function of art in moral culture, — these and other characteristic ideas have assured Schiller an honorable place in the history of modern philosophy. Nowhere is Schiller's historical importance more dramatically displayed than in his criticism of the Kantian ethics. His lasting merit in this connection is that he reassigned to desire a central place in the moral life: desire, not in the sense of an isolated and unbridled impulse, seeking satisfaction in the nearest way, but desire chastened and rationalized, *i. e.*, taking its place in a universe of desire, whose object will be a moral object just in proportion as the æsthetic and social culture of the individual has been deepened and completed. A man is moral, not in proportion as he has succeeded in defeating impulse in obedience to reason, as Kant seemed to hold, but rather as he has rationalized and refined impulse, which thereupon has unrestricted play. Not inclination and duty, but inclination to duty, is the ideal constitution of man. "Even in the purest manifestation of the divine part of his nature," Schiller says in an oft-quoted passage, "man must not leave the sensuous behind. He must not found the triumph of the one upon the suppression of the other. Only when action flows from his entire humanity as the result of the united action of both principles, when it has become second nature to him, is his morality secure."[94] Thus is the autonomy of the moral life established. "An enemy who is only overpowered and cast down can rise again, but the enemy who is reconciled is truly vanquished."

The relation of Schiller to the more strictly metaphysical views of Kant and his successors, however, is a subject to which only scant attention has been given by historians of philosophy, and which is frequently ill understood or entirely misapprehended.[95] There are two reasons for this. In the first place, Schiller's interest in metaphysical questions was entirely subordinate to his interest in ethical and æsthetical problems. Even in his early writings, where the metaphysical interest is strong, the human bearings of metaphysical problems are almost invariably in the background of his consciousness, and are often explicitly traced out. In the later periods of his thought, his theoretical reflections centered more and more around those social and human problems with which as a poet he was primarily concerned, — the problems of the relation of the individual to society, of beauty and duty, of freedom and necessity, of art and moral culture.

In the second place, Schiller's metaphysical views, in so far as he can be said to have held metaphysical views in any serious way, did not constitute a clear development upon those of Kant, as did his ethical and æsthetic theories. The line of philosophical progress doubtless lay in the direction of absolute idealism. One of the central problems of post-Kantian metaphysical and epistemological speculation was to introduce unity into the Kantian system by the expulsion or the assimilation of Kant's thing-in-itself, which, to use the striking word of

Hegel, hovered like a pale ghost about the Kantian system. To this end the philosophical efforts of Fichte, Schelling and Hegel were alike directed. But with this main movement of post-Kantian philosophy, as I shall seek to show, Schiller was never in any significant way identified.

Whether Schiller remained to the end a true Kantian in his metaphysical views, or whether he should rather be classed with the post-Kantians, is a problem for the solution of which materials in the shape of systematic philosophical writings from Schiller's hand are unfortunately rather meager, the *Letters on Æsthetic Education* having been partly worked out before Fichte's influence upon Schiller made itself distinctly felt. The fact that Schiller had been for three years almost exclusively occupied with the study of Kant, and that the period of his active philosophical study and productivity was drawing to a close, is not without interest in the present connection.

In the absence of a large amount of systematic material upon the basis of which to estimate Fichte's influence upon Schiller, the epistolary literature of the period becomes of special significance. There are a number of letters which are of particular interest not only because they throw light upon the personal relations between Fichte and Schiller, but also because they contain passages of first importance for the determination of Schiller's position on some of the fundamental problems of German idealism. The most important of these letters, to enumerate them together, are a letter from Schiller to Körner of June 12, 1794, one by Humboldt to Schiller of September 22, 1794, one by Schiller to Goethe of October 28, 1794, one by Schiller to Hoven of November 21, 1794, and finally the correspondence between Schiller and Fichte of the summer of 1795, especially the letter from Schiller to Fichte, of June 24.

Schiller had met Fichte at Tübingen in the early summer of 1794, when Fichte was on his way to Jena where he was to succeed to the chair of philosophy at the university vacated by Reinhold's removal to the University of Kiel. Their acquaintance became closer through their subsequent professional and personal association at Jena, where Fichte became one of the contributors to Schiller's newly established literary periodical, the *Horen.* That Schiller read the major part of Fichte's writings at this time, including his political tracts, the *Kritik aller Offenbarung*, *Über den Begriff der Wissenschaftslehre*, the *Grundlage der gesammten Wissenschaftslehre*, and the lectures, *Über die Bestimmung des Gelehrten*, all of which were published in 1793 and 1794, is put beyond question by various references in Schiller's correspondence and by clear traces of the influence of these works upon the political ideas, particularly, and upon the general terminology of the first two series of Schiller's *Æsthetic Letters.* The high respect which Fichte's genius inspired in Schiller is clearly shown in Schiller's letter to Körner of June 12, 1794. "Fichte is a most interesting acquaintance," he writes, "more, however, on account of his teachings themselves than his manner. He is doubtless a man of great promise for philosophy." [96] In the letter to Hoven of November 21, 1794, he is still more generous in Fichte's praise. "Since I have been in Jena I have been studying Kantian philosophy again, and have been very happy in it. Fichte interests me also. He is the author of a new system of philosophy which is built upon Kant's and confirms Kant, but which contains much that is new and great in its form. He will doubtless arouse much controversy, but his superior genius will carry everything before it, for he is surely after Kant the greatest speculative intellect of this century.[97]

That Fichte reciprocated the high regard which Schiller expressed for him is indicated by a letter from Humboldt to Schiller which is of the greatest interest to the student of the relation between Fichte and Schiller, not so much because it shows the high esteem in which Fichte held Schiller during the first part of the

Jena period, but because it indicates unmistakably the view which Fichte himself took of Schiller's relation to the Kantian and post-Kantian philosophy at this time. "I had an interesting conversation with Fichte," writes Humboldt;[98] "among other things we talked about yourself. He expects a great deal for philosophy from you. The only thing which your system needs, according to him, is unity, a unity which doubtless exists in your feeling, but which you have as yet not incorporated into your system. If you could only achieve that, you would inaugurate a new epoch in philosophy." The unity, of course, which Fichte had in mind could, according to Fichte's view, be attained only by the abandonment of the Kantian dualism between subject and object, a dualism to which Schiller had unequivocally committed himself, and to which he continued to adhere, and this separated Schiller once and for all from the great movement of philosophical criticism and construction known as post-Kantian idealism.

If Fichte's testimony as to Schiller's philosophical position were not decisive, Schiller's own utterance on the matter in the well known letter to Goethe of October 28, 1794, should establish this position beyond question. After referring to the Kantian spirit pervading the first series of *Æsthetic Letters*, which had just been completed, he expresses his conviction that the fundamental principles of the Kantian philosophy, tacitly recognized from the very beginning of human thought, must ever remain unassailable, which is more, he adds, than can be said of the Fichtean system, according to which the ego is creative, and includes the whole of reality within itself. " The world is a sort of ball, which the ego pitches into space only to catch it again! This is the declaration of divinity which we have been expecting." [99] The passage is of the greatest interest as indicating clearly the fundamental philosophical difference between the two men. The motive of Fichte's *Wissenschaftslehre* from its first inception was the refutation of " dogmatism," the standpoint according to which experience is explained as partly, at least, the product of the non-ego, the thing-in-itself. But Schiller, both in his earlier philosophical period, and at the height of his speculative activity, never abandoned the presupposition of an extra-mental object, the material of sense experience, and the condition of thought and will.

As the æsthetic theories of Fichte and Schiller are intimately bound up with their metaphysical views, we are at once prepared for a certain amount of divergence in their æsthetic opinions. In this connection the correspondence between Schiller and Fichte during the summer of 1795 is of special importance. Fichte had sent Schiller, at the latter's request, a paper, *Über Geist und Buchstab in der Philosophie*,[100] for publication in the *Horen*. Schiller understood the article to be meant as a caricature and a refutation of his own *Æsthetic Letters*, and returned the paper to Fichte, accompanied by a letter in which he criticized both the form and the contents of the Fichte production. The somewhat acrimonious correspondence which followed is of considerable historical importance, inasmuch as it reveals not only certain theoretical differences between the two men, but led to an estrangement between them, which, aggravated by a number of other incidents, prevented any close intimacy in after years.[101]

A point of fundamental difference arises in connection with the analysis of human nature with a view to assigning the place of the æsthetic impulse among the various powers of the soul, an analysis which yields, in Fichte, a primary impulse of self-activity (*Grundtrieb der Selbstthätigkeit*) of which the three impulses, the noetic, which seeks to determine the truth of presentations, the practical, which seeks to realize presentations, and the æsthetic, which finds an interest in presentations for their own sake, are only special or subordinate manifestations. Now the material for this general impulse of self-activity, Fichte contends, is not a given, extra-mental, object, the condition of presentations, as some philosophers erroneously maintain, but is immanent in the impulse itself. It is, in fact, determined by nothing except itself. Schiller's psychological analysis yields, as is well known, two irreducible impulses, the material and the formal (*Stofftrieb* and *Formtrieb*), both, however, implying the existence of an extra-mental object, which acts as the condition for their activity. To the material impulse, Schiller complains particularly,[102] Fichte accords no recognition. The fundamental disagreement between the two men suggested in the letters above presents itself here in another connection. Fichte conceives of matter as self-limitation, a limitation immanent in the impulse of self-activity itself; Schiller, in thoroughly Kantian style, conceives it as an external limit in relation to which alone the self can find the condition for its activity.

Fichte's discussion of the third of his special impulses, the æsthetic, its independence of noetic and practical interests and motives, and its freedom from desire, presents a striking resemblance to the conception of Kant and Schiller, as does also the doctrine developed in Fichte's *Sittenlehre*, concerning æsthetic education. These special æsthetic doctrines, interesting as a comparative study of them would be, do not, however, concern us further, as they throw little additional light upon the metaphysical relations of Schiller to post-Kantianism, which we are here seeking to determine.

The view of the philosophical relations of Schiller to post-Kantianism developed here is apparently contradicted by a remarkable passage in Hegel, to which Mr. Bosanquet has called particular attention in his *History of Æsthetics*.[103] "It is Schiller, then," says Hegel, "to whom we must give credit for the great service of having broken through the Kantian subjectivity and abstraction of thought, and of having ventured to go quite beyond it, by intellectually apprehending unity and reconciliation as the truth, and by making them real through the power of art. Now this unity of the universal and particular, of freedom and necessity, of the spiritual and the natural, which Schiller scientifically conceived as the principle and essence of art, and unweariedly strove to call to life by art and æsthetic culture, was afterwards, under the name of the "Idea," made the principle of knowledge and existence, and pronounced the sole truth and reality. It was by this conception that science attained in Schelling its absolute standpoint." Credit is due to Tomaschek,[104] however, for having shown that Hegel's interpretation of certain passages in Schiller was based upon an imperfect acquaintance with Schiller's thought, an interpretation based upon a superficial reading of the *Æsthetic Letters,* mainly the fourth. It is presumably unnecessary to treat exhaustively what was probably a mere misconception on Hegel's part, and it will perhaps suffice to state that Hegel's error consists in interpreting as a metaphysical theory of reality Schiller's notion of the unity of the spiritual and the natural, the universal and the particular, which was intended by Schiller to be merely an ethical precept or ideal. The organization in man of the rational and the sensuous, which formed such a striking part of Schiller's ethical thought, is falsely taken by Hegel to be the identity of the ideal and the real. These two elements, however, are held in strict separation by Schiller, and Hegel's criticism of Kant, that the latter had not transcended the opposition of subjective thought and objective reality, applies to Schiller as fully as it does to Kant.

That the notion of unity and reconciliation was to Schiller merely one of anthropological and ethical significance, an *Idee der Menschheit,* is further shown by the fact, already referred to in the preceding chapter, that it is conceived by Schiller not as an actual condition, but rather as an ideal to be striven for, an ideal which art might be instrumental in aiding to realize more and more completely. The ideal of a completed humanity is, indeed, forever beyond the reach of human fulfilment. "It is indeed demanded of man," he says in *Anmut und Würde*, "to bring about a complete union of his two natures, and to form an harmonious whole, so as to act with his entire humanity. But this beauty of character, the last fruit of his humanity, is but an idea, for the realization of which he may strive with constant vigilance, but which with all his efforts he can never completely attain." And again, in the *Æsthetic Letters:* "This reciprocal relation between the two impulses (the material and the formal) is indeed only a task of reason, which man is able to accomplish only in the perfection of his being. It is in the strictest signification of the term the idea of his humanity, an infinite goal to which he may approach nearer and nearer, in the progress of time, but without ever reaching it."[105]

That the above is probably the correct view of the real relation of Schiller to post-Kantian idealism may be seen from the following passage taken from one of his letters to Humboldt written in 1805, in which he expresses his fidelity to the Kantian philosophy, and his lack of sympathy with its subsequent developments. "Speculative philosophy," he says, "if it ever attracted me, has disgusted me with its empty forms; I found no living springs and nothing to nourish me on its barren plain; but the deep fundamental ideas of the idealistic philosophy are an abiding treasure, and, if only on their account, we must count ourselves happy to have lived in this age."

It is hardly necessary, after all that has been said, to dwell upon the merits and shortcomings of the philosophy we have endeavored to outline in the various stages of its development. That Schiller was not a systematic thinker those who have tried most diligently to follow his lines of thought have doubtless had the best opportunity to find out. But it is not always true that the thinker who gives himself up most completely to system will have the truest insight, as the philosopher whom Schiller found it necessary to criticize abundantly illustrates. With a power of logical analysis and a love for abstraction such as perhaps no other man has ever possessed, Kant divided and subdivided to a degree such that it took a generation of thinkers to weld together and infuse life into the reality which he had broken up and left lying in fragments, only externally and mechanically related to each other. Now it is the main merit of Schiller (1) that he saw, perhaps more clearly than anyone else in his time, that human nature, at least, in which he was mainly interested, was not a mere aggregate of parts, a house divided against itself, but an organic whole, and that he attempted to base ethics not on this or that part or power of the whole, but upon human nature is its entirety; (2) that he viewed morality not as something complete or static, but as a slow growth, influenced by and bound up with the broader stream of natural and historical evolution, directed more or less consciously, of course, by human education. He emphasized (3) the possibility of this moral education through the refinement of man's æsthetic nature by means of the objects of æsthetic appreciation, and he himself became a distinguished leader in moral and political reform by the products, not often surpassed in imaginative sweep and artistic finish, of his poetic activity. But if Schiller still belabors the reader with a cumbrous and pedantic vocabulary, and often struggles helplessly in the meshes of certain Kantian distinctions which do not any longer engage the interests of educated men, if he still goes back to the water-tight compartments of the human mind, after the manner of his school, or believes in idyllic states of nature in a faraway past that our larger historical knowledge has taught us to put by as poetic fictions, we must not let his faults blind us to his virtues and his real service to philosophy. They only serve to show again that philosophy is itself a product of slow growth, and that no man, no matter how distinguished his talents or how great his industry, can entirely escape the imperfections and shortcomings even of the systems he undertakes to criticize.

Notes

Notes

[1] Henry Jones, *Browning as a Philosophical and Religious Teacher,* p. 15.

[2] Caird, *Evolution of Religion,* Vol. I, p. 315.

[3] *Reason in Religion,* p. 9.

[4] For an excellent discussion of the relations between literature and philosophy, cf. Taylor, *Elements of Metaphysics,* p. 5 ff.

[5] Browning, *The Ring and the Book,* I.

[6] Tennyson, *The Ancient Sage.*

[7] Cf. Ralph Barton Perry, *Harvard Theological Review,* April, 1909.

[8] Windelband, *Geschichte d. neueren Philosophie,* Vol. II, p. 248.

[9] For titles, see the bibliography at the end of this book.

[10] James Seth, *Ethical Principles,* p. 16.

[11] *The Problems of Philosophy,* p. 162.

[12] For further confirmation of the view of the historical significance of Schiller presented see Höffding, *History of Modern Philosophy,* Vol. II, 122, 130 ff.; Hettner, *Gesch. d. d. Literatur, Drittes Buch, Erster Abschnitt, Zweite Abteilung,* 141 ff.; Paulsen, *System of Ethics,* Introduction.

[13] K. Berger, *Entwickelung v. Schiller's Aesthetik.*

[14] The reader who desires a fuller knowledge of Leibniz should consult Duncan, Leibniz, *Philosophical Works;* Russell, *A Critical Exposition of the Philosophy of Leibniz;* Merz, *Leibniz;* and the histories of philosophy, especially Falckenberg, Erdmann and Kuno Fischer. For the philosophy of the entire period see also the excellent recent work by Professor Hibben, *The Philosophy of the Enlightment.*

[15] For Shaftesbury, see v. Gizycki, *Die Philosophie Shaftesburys;* Fowler, *Shaftesbury and Hutcheson,* and the histories of philosophy.

[16] For an interesting discussion of the relation of egoism to altruism consult Spencer, *Data of Ethics,* chapters XI-

XIV; Paulsen, *System of Ethics,* Book II, chapter VI; Sorley, *The Ethics of Naturalism,* and other treatises on ethics.

[17] Wundt, *Ethics,* Vol. II, p. 74.

[18] Compare Sidgwick, *History of Ethics,* pp. 201-204.

[19] *Essays on the Passions,* p. 17. Quoted by Mackintosh, *Ethical Philosophy,* p. 126.

[20] For an attractive discussion of this important point see Paulsen, *A System of Ethics,* Book II, chapter V.

[21] See on this point Höffding, *Problems of Philosophy,* pp. 169 and 197, and his *Ethik;* also Taylor, *The Problem of Conduct,* chapter IV, especially p. 201 ff.; Bradley, *Appearance and Reality,* p. 414 ff.; and the literature on egoism and altruism cited above.

[22] James Seth, *Ethical Principles,* p. 18.

[23] For a similar objection in the theory of education see Bagley, *The Educative Process,* p. 50 ff.

[24] For a detailed and highly interesting account of Schiller's studies in the Stuttgart Academy, see Minor, *Schiller,* I, p. 192-292.

[25] Karl Gödeke, *Schiller's sämmtliche Schriften, historisch-kritische Ausgabe,* Stuttgart, I, 74-94. Unless otherwise specified, all references will be to this standard edition of Schiller's complete works. For other editions and bibliography, consult the bibliography at the end of the book.

[26] The essay was originally in five chapters, but only a part of the first chapter has come down to us. Efforts have been made to restore the lost portions from the criticisms of Consbruch, Schiller's instructor in medicine, which are extant. Fortunately, Schiller has made this work rather unnecessary, as the gist of the paper is doubtless repeated in Schiller's second master's dissertation, *On the Connection between the Animal and the Spiritual Nature in Man,* to be discussed presently.

[27] *Schriften,* I, pp. 75-6.

[28] Cf. Chapter VIII.

[29] Weber, *History of Philosophy,* p. 320. For a thorough discussion of the various theories of the relation between soul and body consult Taylor, *Elements of Metaphysics,* Book IV, chapter II, and literature cited there.

[30] Minor, *Schiller,* I, 257.

[31] Little progress has been made, in spite of the enormous advance of the science of neurology, in the solution

of this interesting problem of the conversion of physical processes successively into nerve processes and thence into processes of consciousness. For a modern discussion of this subject, see Donaldson, The Central Nervous System, in the *American Text-Book of Physiology,* especially pp. 232-33; Hering, *Zur Theorie der Nerventhätigkeit;* Wundt, *Physiological Psychology;* Ebbinghaus, *Psychologie,* I, p. 144, and literature cited there.

[32] Wundt, *Physiological Psychology,* ii, p. 387.

[33] James, *Principles of Psychology,* ii, pp. 561, 564.

[34] Cf. Minor, *op. cit.,* i, p. 279.

[35] *Schiller in seinem Verhältnisse zur Wissenschaft.* Wien, 1862.

[36] *Schriften,* i, p. 143.

[37] *Schriften,* i, p. 143.

[38] *Schriften,* i, p. 152.

[39] *Schriften,* i, p. 156.

[40] *Schriften,* i, p. 156.

[41] *Schriften,* i, p. 158.

[42] *Schriften,* i, p. 154.

[43] *Schriften,* i, p. 159 ff.

[44] *Schriften,* i, p. 170.

[45] *Schriften,* ii, pp. 340-48; iii, pp. 509-24.

[46] January, 1782.

[47] A distinct advance upon the principle of nature imitation of Sulzer and Mendelssohn, which Schiller had himself recently expressed in the first preface to the *Robbers,* is noticed here. Cf. Schiller's idea with Lessing's *Dramaturgie,* Part 2, letter 79.

[48] Cf. Tomaschek, *op. cit.,* p. 25; Überweg, *Schiller als Historiker und Philosoph,* p. 70; Berger, *op. cit.,* p. 34.

[49] *Schriften,* iii, 523.

[50] A first-hand knowledge of Shaftesbury at this period is improbable, as appears from a letter to Lotte von Lengefeld of November 27th, 1788, in which he "hopes to enjoy Shaftesbury; perhaps he would give him pastime in the summer." See Tomaschek, *op. cit.,* p. 15, n. 10. For a more detailed discussion of influences, see Palleske, *Schiller's Leben und Werke,* I, p. 76 ff., p. 100 ff., and II, p. 180 ff.; also Boas, *Schiller's Jugendjahre,* p. 136 ff.

[51] Cf. Tomaschek, *op. cit.,* p. 10 and note 31.

[52] For the influence of Leibniz's theory of presentation upon subsequent sense physiology, see Sommer, *Deutsche Psychologie und Aesthetik,* p. 51 ff., p. 368.

[53] *Life of Schiller,* p. 53.

[54] *Schiller's Leben,* ii, p. 39.

[55] For various opinions regarding the dates of their composition, cf. Tomaschek, *op. cit.,* p. 31, n. 11. Nevinson's date (autumn, 1785) is almost certainly a year too late.

[56] Cf. p. 37 f.

[57] *Freigeisterei der Leidenschaft, Schriften,* iv, p. 23 ff. Hempel's tr.

[58] *Journal of Speculative Philosophy,* xii, p. 379.

[59] The *Philosophical Letters,* of which there are five in all, three by *Julius* and two by *Raphael,* were published in the *Thalia,* the first four in 1786, the last not until 1789. This was answered by Schiller, April 15, 1788. Cf. *Correspondence of Schiller and Körner,* tr. Simpson, i, p. 217.

[60] *Schiller als Philosoph,* p. 59. Cf. also *Schiller's Jugend- und Wanderjahre in Selbstbekenntnissen,* pp. 245-6.

[61] Whether the document is too mature to be accounted for by this supposition, as Harnack would seem to maintain, is a point which affords opportunity for the nicest literary discrimination, but which, it seems to me, must remain largely a matter of individual opinion.

[62] *Schriften,* iv, p. 59.

[63] *Schriften,* iv, pp. 36-7.

[64] *Schriften,* iv, p. 54.

[65] *Schriften,* iv, pp. 59-60.

[66] *Correspondence of Schiller and Körner,* tr. Simpson, i, pp. 131-2.

[67] Letter to Körner, Aug. 29th, 1787.

[68] For Schiller's philosophical friends and associates cf. Tomaschek, *op. cit.,* p. 143 ff.

[69] *Life of Schiller,* p. 88.

[70] *Correspondence with Körner, Ibid.,* ii, 172. Many other quotations from Schiller, *pro* and *con,* might be made. Cf. his letters to Humboldt, June 27, 1798; to Körner, Dec. 10, 1804; to Goethe, Oct. 16, 1795; and to Rochlitz, April 16, 1801.

[71] *Life of Schiller,* p. 100.

[72] *Correspondence with Körner,* tr. Simpson, ii, p. 204.

[73] Hoffmeister, Meurer, and others.

[74] *Correspondence with Körner,* ed. Veit., ii, pp. 187, 192.

[75] Cf. Schiller's letter to Körner, Dec. 4, 1791. The date given by Kuno Fischer is incorrect.

[76] *Correspondence with Körner,* Veit. ed., ii, pp. 167-8. Cf. Tomaschek, p. 254, n. 37.

[77] Cf. *Wallenstein,* pt. iii, act ii, sc. 2.

[78] *Schriften,* x, pp. 92-3.

[79] Cf. *Schriften,* x, 79, note.

[80] Cf. *Schriften,* x, pp. 95-6.

[81] *Schriften,* x, 97.

[82] *Schriften,* x, 101.

[83] *Schiller's Briefwechsel mit Körner,* Gödeke ed., iii, pp. 42-3.

[84] *Schriften,* x, p. 100.

[85] Besides *Anmut und Würde,* see *Über das Pathetische, Grund des Vergnügens an tragischen Gegenständen, Tragische Kunst,* and *Über den moralischen Nutzen aesthetischer Sitten.*

[86] *Einleitung in die Moralwissenschaft,* i, p. 220.

[87] *An einen jungen Freund als er sich der Weltweisheit widmete.* The translation of this and the following poems is by Sir Bulwer Lytton.

[88] Cf. *Anmut und Würde, Schriften,* x, pp. 109-110. See also Jodl, *loc. cit.*

[89] *Schriften,* x, p. 117.

[90] *Schriften,* x, pp. 229-230.

[91] *Aesthetische Briefe,* 23.

[92] Cf. Windelband, *Geschichte der neueren Philosophie,* Vol. II, p. 260 ff.

[93] I speak here of the Christian religion, as being that which has had perhaps the most general influence among the civilized nations.

[94] *Anmut und Würde.*

[95] Cf. for the whole subject, Tomaschek, *op. cit.,* Book V.

[96] Jonas, *Schiller's Briefe,* III, p. 453.

[97] Jonas, *op. cit.,* IV, p. 69.

[98] *Schiller's u. Humboldt's Briefwechsel,* 2 ed., p. 57.

[99] *Briefwechsel zwischen Schiller und Goethe,* I, p. 25.

[100] Contained in Fichte's complete *Werke,* Volume VIII.

[101] The Fichte-Schiller correspondence has been published by J. G. Fichte, *Schiller's u. Fichte's Briefwechsel.* See especially p. 28 ff.

[102] See *op. cit.,* p. 31.

[103] P. 287.

[104] *Schiller in seinem Verhältnisse zur Wissenschaft,* p. 438.

[105] *Schriften,* x, p. 320. See also pp. 328-9, 413. Cf. Jodl, *Geschichte der Ethik in der neueren Philosophie,* p. 53 ff.

Bibliography

Bibliography

The extensive Schiller bibliographies in Gödeke, *Grundriss zur Geschichte der deutschen Dichtung,* and in the *Jahresberichte für neuere deutsche Literaturgeschichte* are very general and comprehensive, and are, on that account, of little use to the student of Schiller's reflective thought. The more strictly philosophical literature on Schiller is reported periodically in the *Archiv für Geschichte der Philosophie.* A critical bibliography of the philosophical literature of much value, especially for the relation of Schiller to Kant, is the Kant bibliography by Adickes, published in the *Philosophical Review,* III, 4. Of the most recent publications Überweg-Heinze, *Grundriss der Geschichte der Philosophie,* 10 ed., vol. III, gives a very complete account. The following bibliography aims to give a fairly exhaustive account of the literature in books, monographs, dissertations and programs. No attempt has been made to cover with any completeness the periodical literature, except in the case of the few articles written in English.

The philosophical writings of Schiller will be found in complete form and arranged in chronological order in the standard edition of Schiller's complete works, Gödeke, *Schiller's sämmtliche Schriften, historisch-kritische Ausgabe,* Stuttgart, 1868-76. They have recently been published separately in selections by Eugen Kühnemann, *Schiller's philosophische Schriften und Gedichte* (*Auswahl*), Leipzig, 1902; 2 ed., 1910. An English translation of the philosophical works is published in the Bohn Library, London, 1875. Schiller's correspondence has been published in many editions. The most recent and valuable is that of F. Jonas, *Schillers Briefe, Kritische Gesammtausgabe,* Stuttgart, 1892 ff. Of the Schiller biographies perhaps the most important for the philosophical student are those of Hoffmeister and Grün. The very detailed works of Brahm, Weltrich, and Minor, are, unfortunately, incomplete. The demand for a detailed modern life of Schiller has recently been met by two excellent works, Kühnemann's Schiller, and the work of Berger. Calvin Thomas' *The Life and Works of Schiller* also contains an interesting chapter, in a popular vein, on Schiller's philosophy.

Among the best brief treatments of Schiller's philosophy are those found in the standard histories of philosophy and of literature. The chapters in the works of Höffding, Jodl and Windelband, cited below, are in every way admirable. The treatment of the subject by Hettner, *Literaturgeschichte,* though not written by a technical student of philosophy, is one of the most illuminating short discussions of Schiller's philosophical writings which we possess. Of the single works on Schiller as a philosopher mentioned below the titles by Tomaschek, Überweg, Twesten, Zimmermann, Meurer, Hemsen, Drobisch and Fischer are of the first importance. The remainder are either less significant or negligible.

Baltzer, *Schiller, besonders in seiner religiösen Bedeutung,* Gotha, 1860.

Bartsch, *Schiller's Glaube an die Unsterblichkeit der Seele,* Berlin, 1860.

Baumeister, *Über Schiller's Lebensansicht, insbesondere in ihrer Bedeutung zur Kant'schen,* Tübingen, 1897.

Benard, *L'esthetique de Schiller,* C. R. Acad. d. Sci. Mor. et Pol., XXIII, 1870.

Berger, *Die Entwickelung von Schiller's Aesthetik,* Weimar, 1894.

Berger, *Schiller, sein Leben u. seine Werke,* München, 1906-9.

Beste, *Goethe's u. Schiller's Religion,* Gotha, 1783.

Binder, *Schiller im Verhältniss zum Christenthum,* Stuttgart, 1839.

Böhme, *Schillerstudien,* Freiberg, 1891.

Borkowsky, *Die Unsterblichkeitslehre Schillers,* Königsberg, 1898.

Brahm, *Schiller,* Berlin, 1888.

Carruth, *The Religion of Friedrich Schiller,* Publ. Mod. Lang. Assn., XIX, 4.

Carus, *Friedrich Schiller,* Chicago, 1905.

Clasen, *Der Wandel in Schiller's Weltanschauung,* Zeitschrift f. Phil. u. phil. Kritik, 1905, 113-39.

Danzel, Th., *Über d. gegenwärtigen Zustand d. Phil. d.*

Kunst u. ihre nächste Aufgabe. In Danzel's gesammelte Aufsätze, Leipzig, 1855.

Danzel, *Schiller's Briefwechsel mit Körner,* the same.

Drobisch, W., *Über d. Stellung Schillers zur Kantischen Ethik.* In Ber. über d. Verh. d. königlich-sächsischen Ges. d. Wiss. zu Leipzig. Philologisch-hist. Classe. Fifth series, XI, 1860.

Fischer, K., *Schiller als Philosoph,* 2 ed., Heidelberg, 1891.

Fischer, *Schiller als Komiker,* Frkft, 1861.

Foà, A., *L'ideale estetico di F. Schiller,* Parma, 1892.

Frank, A., *Über Schiller's Begriff des sittlich-schönen,* Vienna, 1886.

Friedrich, *Der Glaube Goethes u. Schillers,* Halle, 1891.

Geil, G., *Schillers Ethik u. ihr Verhältniss zu der Kantischen,* Strassburg, 1888.

Geil, G., *System v. Schillers Ethik,* Strassburg, 1890.

Geyer, *Schillers ästhetisch-ethische Weltanschauung,* Berlin, 1898.

Gneisse, K., *Schillers Lehre v. d. ästhetischen Wahrnehmung,* Berlin, 1893.

Grosse, H., *Schillers Briefe über d. ästhetische Erziehung des Menschen u. d. Bedeutung ihres Grundgedankens für d. Pädagogik.* In Mann's Deutsche Blätter für erziehenden Unterricht.

Grün, K., *Schiller als Mensch, Geschichtsschreiber, Denker u. Dichter,* Leipzig, 1844.

Harnack, G. R., *Die klassische Ästhetik der Deutschen,* Leipzig, 1892.

Heine, G., *Das Verhältniss d. Ästhetik z. Ethik bei Schiller,* Leipzig, 1894.

Hemsen, W., *Schillers Ansichten über Schönheit u. Kunst im Zusammenhang gewürdigt,* Göttingen, 1854.

Hettner, H., *Die romantische Schule,* Braunschweig, 1850.

Hettner, H., *Geschichte d. deutschen Literatur im achtzehnten Jahrhundert,* 4 ed., Braunschweig, 1893 ff.

Höffding, H., *History of Modern Philosophy,* tr. Meyer, London, 1900.

Höwe, *Über den vermeintlichen Wechsel in Schillers Ansicht v. Verh. d. Ästh. z. Sittl.,* Dirschau, 1886.

Jodl, F., *Geschichte d. Ethik in d. neueren Philosophie,* Stuttgart, 1882-89.

Jung, *Schiller u. d. Pessimismus,* Meseritz, 1877.

Kuhn, A., *Schillers Geistesgang,* Berlin, 1863.

Kühnemann, E., *Die kantischen Studien Schillers u. d. Komposition d. Wallenstein,* Marburg, 1889.

Kühnemann, E., *Kants u. Schillers Begründung d. Asthetik,* Munich, 1895.

Kühnemann, E., *Schillers philosophische Schriften u. Gedichte* (*Auswahl*), Leipzig, 1902, 2 ed., 1910.

Kühnemann, E., *Schiller,* 3 ed., 1908.

Lange, F. A., *Einleitung u. Kommentar zu Schillers philosophischen Gedichten,* Leipzig, 1897.

Lange, F. A., *History of Materialism,* concluding chapter.

Lange, H., *Schillers philosophische Gedichte,* 2 ed., Berlin, 1905.

Lempp, *Das Problem der Theodicee in d. Phil. u. Lit. d. 18. Jahrh.,* Berlin, 1910.

Liebrecht, L., *Schillers Verhältniss z. Kants ethischer Weltansicht,* Hamburg, 1890.

Lotze, H., *Geschichte d. Ästhetik in Deutschland,* Munich, 1868.

Lübker, *Goethe u. Schiller in ihrem Verh. z. Christenthum,* Hamburg, 1885.

Meier, H., *Welchen Werth haben Schillers Schriften über d. ästhetische Erziehung des Menschen f. d. Pädagogik,* Schleiz, 1879-80.

Meurer, Ch., *Das Verhältniss d. Schillerschen zur Kantischen Ethik,* 2 ed., Leipzig, 1886.

Mensel, *Was verdankt Schiller seinem Kantstudium?* Kiel, 1897.

Minor, *Schiller, sein Leben u. seine Werke,* Berlin, 1890.

Montargis, F., *L'Esthétique de Schiller,* Paris, 1892.

Neudecker, G., *Studien z. Geschichte d. deutschen Ästhetik seit Kant,* Würzburg, 1878.

Neyinson, *Life of Friedrich Schiller,* London, 1889.

Palm, G., *Vergleichende Darstellung von Kants u. Schillers Bestimmungen über das Wesen des Schönen,* Jena, 1878.

Philippson, R., *Die ästhetische Erziehung, ein Beitrag zur Lehre Kants, Schillers u. Herbarts,* Magdeburg, 1890.

Reinitz, E., *Schillers Gedankendichtung in ihrem Verhältniss zur Lehre Kants,* Ratisbon, 1894.

Robertson, *Schiller After a Hundred Years.*

Royce, J., *The Ethical Studies of Schiller,* Journal Spec. Phil., XII, 373 ff.

Schaff, D. S., *Schiller's Religious Views and Influence,* Hom. Rev., vol. 50, 5.

Schmidt, P., *Kant, Schiller, Fischer: Über das Erhabene,* Halle, 1880.

Schnedermann, F., *Ist die Ethik Schillers eine andere nach als vor dem Kantstudium des Dichters?* Leipzig, 1878.

Seidel, *Schillers Glaube,* Dresden, 1883.

Sommer, A., *Über d. Beziehung d. Ansicht Schillers v. Wesen u. d. geistigen Bedeutung d. Kunst zur kantischen Philosophie,* Halle, 1869.

Sommer, R., *Grundzüge einer Geschichte d. deutschen Psychologie u. Ästhetik von Wolff-Baumgarten bis Kant-Schiller,* Würzburg, 1892.

Steiner, *Grundlinien einer Erkenntnisstheorie d. Goetheschen Weltanschauung, mit bes. Rücksicht auf Sch.,* Berlin, 1886.

Tape, *Schiller u. d. praktischen Ideen,* Emden, 1863.

Thikotter, *Ideal u. Leben nach Schiller u. Kant,* Bremen, 1892.

Tomaschek, *Schiller u. Kant,* Vienna, 1857.

Tomaschek, *Schiller in seinem Verhältnisse zur Wissenschaft,* Vienna, 1862.

Twesten, K., *Schiller in seinem Verhältnisse zur Wissenschaft dargestellt,* Berlin, 1863.

Überweg, F., *Schiller als Historiker u. Philosoph,* Leipzig, 1884.

Urlichs, *Schiller u. Fichte,* Deutsche Rundschau, XXXVI, 1883.

Volkmann, F., *Schillers Philosophie,* Berlin, 1899.

Vorländer, K., *Ethischer Rigorismus u. sittliche Schönheit. Mit bes. Rücksicht von Kant u. Schiller,* Phil. Monatshefte, XXX, 225-280; 371-405; 534-577.

Vorländer, K., *Kant, Schiller, Goethe,* Leipzig, 1907.

Walzel, *Schillers Werke, Säkular Ausgabe,* XI, Stuttgart, 1905, Introduction.

Weltrich, *Schiller,* Stuttgart, 1899.

Windelband, W., *Geschichte d. neueren Philosophie,* 1878 ff.

Zimmermann, G., *Versuch einer Schiller Ästhetik,* Leipzig, 1889.

Zimmermann, R., *Ästhetik, Erster, historisch-kritischer Theil,* Vienna, 1858.

Zimmermann, R., *Schiller als Denker.* In *Studien u. Kritiken z. Philosophie u. Ästhetik,* Vienna, 1870.